The New Modernist House

For my mother, the unassuming Modernist.

This book was written and compiled on the
unceded land of the Wadawurrung people.

The New Modernist House

Mid-Century Homes Renewed
for Contemporary Living

Patricia Callan

Contents

← The dimensions of Fender House impart
an aura of the monumental, while new
velour carpet reasserts 1970s nostalgic
warmth. Photography: Derek Swalwell.

Foreword

Hannah Lewi

I grew up in a modern house that was designed by the architect Dennis Silver and constructed in the early 1960s in a suburb of Perth, Western Australia. My parents, as migrants who left the drab postwar northern hemisphere in search of the new, were inspired by the demonstration houses built at the Commonwealth Games Village in Floreat Beach, Perth, in 1962. They asked Silver, who had designed some of the prototype houses, to do something similar on a bush block running down to the Swan River. Like many of his contemporaries, Silver was inspired by what was happening in modern architecture in North and South America, Japan and Europe and received this stimulation through travel and work overseas, the circulation of journals and photographs, and the coming of internationally trained designers to Australia's growing cities.

This modest family home is still standing and has evolved over six decades. That is not to say that there haven't been problems over the years, such as asbestos sheet roofing that is best left well alone, the upkeep of jarrah timber beams and window frames, the replacement of worn rush matting and cork floor tiles, and leaking straw board ceilings that are a nightmare. Inserting wiring and services in the thin-skinned, lean construction is an ongoing struggle. As an architecture student and graduate with little work, I cut my teeth on various small projects throughout the house that were, in hindsight, hit-and-miss: bathroom updates because glass mosaics rarely last the distance; a terraced, walled front garden that is now totally impractical; screen doors and Mondrian-inspired glazed kitchen cupboards designed and made with a builder friend who taught me how to weld in his backyard workshop.

My point is that our houses should be designed well from the outset but can also be coaxed along over the years and left to evolve and mature in their own idiosyncratic ways. Inspired restorations and renovations can deal with this ageing process and with the whims of fashion that are usually salvageable at a later date. It is this approach that should become the mainstay of domestic architectural practice – dealing with the existing rather than an assumed *tabula rasa*. This book is a fine demonstration of how good contemporary design, by varied practices from the young to the established, can solve problems, work within heritage constraints and sensitively resuscitate Australia's postwar housing stock and bring renewed delight.

The New Modernist House shows how subsequent generations can make their own mark without losing the intrinsic value and design essence of the original houses. The homes in this book have been carefully selected from city and regional locations. Some are quite modest, introverted and born from a DIY culture, or reflect the now sadly out of reach democratic ethos of modern house provision for all in postwar suburbs. Others are far more lavish and glam, and have been treated with the exacting, bespoke care they deserve – now humming again to the tunes of Dave Brubeck on the carefully restored record player. (Brubeck was a great enthusiast of the Modernist style, building two mid-century homes designed by Beverley David Thorne).

Australia looked increasingly away from Britain and towards a more optimistic America in the mid-20th century. Programs such as the Case Study Houses initiated by John Entenza and *Arts & Architecture* magazine from 1945 to the mid-1960s – with some twenty of the original built schemes still surviving – were incredibly effective at demonstrating modern domestic design. The architects, which included well-known names like Ray and Charles Eames, Richard Neutra, Craig Ellwood and Pierre Koenig but also many other lesser known too, all embraced experimentation with methods of construction and structural systems. They were characterised by the expression of industrial materials, efficient plans and an informal disposition. The influence on American and Australian housing was huge and clearly still resonates today.

All the selected houses display a sympathy for robust material palettes in brick, concrete and terrazzo, steel or timber frame, and stone or timber panelling. It is the materials that do most of the work to create texture, mood, pattern and tempo without resorting to 'featurism'. Details and junctions are not covered with skirtings and decorative mouldings, and colours are bold and playful or subtle and moody but never 'greige'. Other common traits include a great attention to the flow from inside to outside and a transparency that frames the gardens and landscapes beyond. They have open and flexible plans but they are never totally un-programmed blank white boxes; rather there is a careful sculpting of rooms through changes in ceiling heights, floor levels and structural rhythm. We can imagine our everyday lives being enriched by them – from lounging in the sunken snug to sunbathing on the patio.

Despite the loss of much postwar building stock, there are still many more remaining houses which are great examples of how Australian design has always been able to mediate deftly between international styles and local conditions of climate, context and situation. Publications such as this book are so important in winning over more hearts and minds towards the wider appreciation of mid-century houses, as are design magazines and exhibitions, walking tours and open house days, websites like *Modernist Australia*, and *The Modern House* in the UK, and organisations like DOCOMOMO and the Robin Boyd Foundation. Just like the houses in the Commonwealth Games Village in Perth that were so enthusiastically visited, or the popularity of the Small Homes Service in Australia, there is nothing quite as persuasive as seeing physical demonstrations of what can be done with inspired design.

In addressing the demands of sustainability, the mantra of 'the greenest building is the one already built' is only half true: as these houses show, there is much careful work needed to bring them up to the expectations of current environmental performance.[1] And bespoke houses are just the first step. Greater challenges lie ahead in demonstrating how higher density and public housing (Torbrek being the only apartment in the book), and community and civic buildings can also be renovated, adapted and re-used sympathetically and yet with forward-thinking about how our future built environments need to perform to meet environmental, urban and climate challenges head-on. That is the pressing task ahead for architects, builders, clients and educators alike.

Hannah Lewi

Hannah Lewi is a Professor of Architecture in the Melbourne School of Design at the University of Melbourne and co-director of the Australian Centre for Architecture History and Urban and Cultural Heritage. She is vice-chair of DOCOMOMO Australia, and author of a number of publications, including *Australia Modern: Architecture, Landscape and Design*, Thames & Hudson, 2019.

1   The website *Australian Architects Declare Climate & Biodiversity Emergency* has received over 1100 signatories. Point number 6 states: 'Upgrade existing buildings for extended use as a more carbon efficient alternative to demolition and new build whenever there is a viable choice.' See <au.architectsdeclare.com>.

Introduction

Patricia Callan

A 1969 McGlashan Everist-designed home in Geelong suburbia was my childhood universe – a Spielbergian dreamscape on the edge, where housing development fell away to the golden steppe of Western Victoria. Here, rambling homes of green shag carpet and split levels recalling *The Brady Bunch* still abound. Further variations of domestic living filled my childhood: the modest cream brick, three-bedroom homes of my primary school friends, my grandmother's postwar apartment building with its floating terrazzo stairs, and the pastel beach shacks of the nearby Surf Coast, the perennial scene of teenage shenanigans. Altogether it was a very middle-class, late 20th-century context, with each aesthetic burrowing into my psyche in its own way.

To be artsy in 1990s regional Australia was to live the norm but be unceasingly on the lookout for the 'other' – music, style, people. As a mid-teen, already op-shopping weekly and well on the way to loitering in art studios for the next decade (I later studied sculpture and ceramic design in Melbourne), I chanced upon a Brashs bargain bin copy of *Compact Jazz: Best of Bossa Nova*[1] that assumed immediate high rotation alongside The Breeders and The Jon Spencer Blues Explosion. The lilting exotica as cooed by Astrud Gilberto and friends fused with my collection of once-discarded relics (mostly homewares and clothes) embodying the 1950s and 60s design rules of my parents' generation. I was not alone in this revival, but rather one of a swathe who arrived at Mid-Century Modern design appreciation not through formal study, but via pop culture. My education in Modernist architecture specifically coalesced in remembrance of the elemental pleasures of my childhood home – the timber scent, the warm light, the aural softness – and a rather naive revelation, once leaving home, that most houses in Australia are deficient in the specific sensory joys that are gained from design, by design.

With the arrival of the internet and an ascendant housing boom, my online real estate explorations began to rival the epic jags of gamers. An accelerating appreciation of Mid-Century Modernist architecture fuelled my internal fury as beautiful, sometimes high-pedigree buildings were sold by unapologetic spivs for nothing but land and immediately destroyed. Of course, there was only one thing to do about this situation in 2007 PS (Pre-Socials): I had to blog about it. And so modernistaustralia.com was born. Sourcing obvious Mid-Century Modernist homes for sale in any condition, I published these images in my own 'listings'. I celebrated their design attributes and histories. I encouraged the retention of these buildings via a lens of potential and did not hold back in deriding those who championed their destruction. At the outset, my intention for the blog was merely as a vehicle to vent my frustration.

However, over time, engagement crept across many quarters as I frankly, sometimes foolishly, dissected, praised and savaged house listings across the country. Design aficionados, real estate agents and even mid-century architects' families weighed in as modernistaustralia.com converted real estate marketing into an entry point for public discussion on our unfairly maligned architectural heritage. The site and subsequent social media presence prodded a previously unexplored flank of community building, creating a forum more accessible and colloquial than architectural academia or heritage regulation might achieve. The presiding theory emerged that if by extolling their virtues, Mid-Century Modernist residences grew in desirability, and that if money is the final arbiter in the longevity of a building, then driving desire increases the dollar, that maybe some of these homes could be saved. After thousands of listings, countless homes 'rescued' via purchase by sympathetic buyers and fifteen years, I think it's made a valuable contribution to expanding the appreciation of Australia's Mid-Century Modernist architecture overall.

Over these same years, my vaguely maturing online persona and desire to get out of the city with my young family conspired in our own Hail Mary bid on a 1970s beach town Modernist house, designed by Eoin Barnett. The home in question was a humble affair yet expressly vibrated with architectural discipline: northern orientation, flat roofline, concrete block construction and internal timber ceilings. It was the home of the architect himself, a generous man, serendipitously influenced by the self-same firm McGlashan Everist of my childhood home. The impetus for us to buy the residence was immediate, as circling rivals mulled painting the block-work and other destructive threats hung in the air. We were overcome with a searing need to ensure the building's integrity and thoroughly enjoy its crafted details, spaces and irreplaceable materials. Seven years after its purchase, we locked in the decision to extend and refurbish this now forty-year-old home, a project completed within the unforeseen plot-twist of the global covid pandemic.

Though I am not in any formal sense an expert, our process of renovating this architect-designed Mid-Century Modern 'forever' home brought to bear many untested concepts around lifestyle architecture, practicality and environment, and I have touched on these results in the essay on page 12. There I also traverse a basic narrative of Modernist design to set some historical and cultural bearings. I hope these ideas and histories hold a common interest for anyone approaching similar projects.

This book is primarily a celebration of those Mid-Century Modern residences across Australia that have been sympathetically renovated and updated for contemporary living. *The New Modernist House* explores twenty-one excellent examples from across the nation, ordered chronologically according to the original build. These projects embrace extraordinary variation, including a three-bed Torbreck Apartment by Job & Froud Architects (1960) in Highgate Hill, renovated by KIN Architects with space-age glamour (see page 126); Alistair Knox's rustic Fisher House (1969) in Warrandyte, sensitively updated by Adriana Hanna (see page 216); and Peter Green & Associates' suburban beauty (1979) in Bridgeman Downs, reorientated by Cloud Dwellers in a tonal piquancy of Bismark Blue (see page 254).

Since the turn of the 21st century, Australia has experienced an enormous upswing in renovation culture with the accompanying saturation of television shows, social media and neighbourly chatter. Separate from this, appreciation of Mid-Century Modernist architecture and design has cycled in, albeit via more niche avenues. These two cultural juggernauts have collided in a multitude of ways, though the former does not necessarily support the latter. That said, the residences in this book stand as an inspiration in both categories. Each residence profiled is a sliver of local architecture in which the Mid-Century Modern principles that inform its design have been embraced, deeply considered and beautifully reimagined through its renovation. With great creativity and expertise, every owner and their practitioners deliberately set out to elevate their home's architectural origins and neighbourhood character, recasting the elusive light and relaxed atmosphere of its Mid-Century Modern spaces into contemporary usefulness. Each place contains its own story and stands as truly contemporary, reflecting the owner's personality just as much as its architectural taxonomy.

Our national obsession with renovation likely stems from the worrisome yet presiding ideology of housing as an investment vehicle. In Kate Wagner's excellent essay, 'How Beige Took Over American Homes', she posits that in the early 21st century housing became hijacked by 'the market', which utterly changed renovation projects and the very concept of a home:

> After centuries of the home being primarily a place or a space, during the 2000s it was seen as primarily an object or, more specifically, an asset. At a time where mortgage speculation made our houses disposable and impermanent, beige slipped happily onto the walls of millions of Americans, who wanted easy ways to make their house 'worth more' at the behest of HGTV and other media, who treated the home as a thing to be changed, or disposed of on a whim.[2]

Introduction

70 Reigate Road, 1979

We used to speed down the 3-step split level
hallway in our socks trying to slide across the
tiled floor all the way to the kitchen's end.

Eliza Gosse

Patricia Callan

This situation is perhaps more acute in Australia, with the beige in Wagner's example swapped out for white and cool grey. Any home of architectural merit or liveability can fall victim to this disposable 'improvement' mentality, which, apart from a dire waste of resources, may destroy instances of incredible craft and extinguishes our communal links to local narratives and environments.

In selecting the homes and creative effort featured in this book, each one emerged to embody four fundamentals: retention, camaraderie, longevity and contemporary focus. These shared values wind through the twenty-one projects, binding all in this new tradition of sympathetic Mid-Century Modern renovation.

Retention

Each project undertakes specific acts of salvage and repurposing to ensure that rare or expensive materials, crafted detail and character remain as part of the overall project. The embrace of sustainable practices and rejection of cavalier wastefulness is an underlying imperative for these architects, owners and builders.

Camaraderie

Mid-Century Modernism is a community unto itself and the adoring collective embrace of these houses and their histories is found everywhere: from savvy real estate agents who champion a property's continued future over a quick land sale to architects who relish the opportunity to work around the boundaries of their creative forebears and sage builders who revere long-lost craftsmanship.

Longevity

Several of these renovations came in the aftermath of a deceased estate sale. Some were intergenerational transfers. Other owners had already lived in their homes for years, expressing no desire to leave but simply reorient. This is the real-world actualisation of the overused term 'forever house'. Beautiful design for life is never more manifest than in buildings that are continually inhabited by a single family for many years or which are never sold, in life, by their owners.

Contemporary focus

Those who love these homes have an implicit understanding that true Modernist buildings are designed around ideas, not a slavish dedication to a 'look'. Contained in each brief to the practitioners who realised these projects, to a greater or lesser extent, stands the sentiment: 'The owners do not wish to create a "retro" museum or set piece, but a more useful, comfortable home.' Though personal tastes and familial circumstances differ wildly, each house we see here is altered for living *today*. The homes, while totally informed by the past, are not precious shrines to long-dead eras or architects, and that is what makes them, in all their variations, an utter inspiration.

Aiming to repair and update with integrity, underscored by these values, increases a building's longevity in all metrics and ultimately retains its inherently wonderful character. That is where all the projects in this book find their beginning and achieve brilliant success at their end.

I hope the following pages of glorious homes, gracious owners and consummate creativity introduce you to an array of practical pathways and cultural rabbit holes – or perhaps propel your own curiosity and appreciation of Mid-Century Modernism, adding another welcome body to our expanding community that cherishes this architecture in all its forms.

1   Polygram Records, 1987.

2   Kate Wagner, 'How Beige Took Over American Homes', *Atlas Obscura*, 26 September 2016.

Mid-Century Modernism:
Beginnings and Legacy

Patricia Callan

To wholly appreciate the new creative work that deftly celebrates and expands upon the original architecture of the homes in this book, it is valuable to have some knowledge of where Mid-Century Modernism began and the influences that shaped its rise. Without wandering into any philosophical fight clubs, this essay traverses a basic narrative of Modernist architecture and design to set some historical and cultural bearings.

In addition to this, the next section draws on my own experiences of observing, living in and renovating a Mid-Century Modern home, with some practical musings around 'sympathetic' renovation in contemporary Australia. This section examines subjects such as understanding your home and your personal needs for the project, working with professional practitioners, ecological responsibility, design challenges and safety considerations.

What is Mid-Century Modernism, anyway?

In the context of the home, Modernism is a socially informed way of building spaces and items for living according to need and function. It can be best described as a cluster of design ideals, born at the start of the 20th century. These ideals reeled away from the ornate excesses of the preceding Victorian era and reacted to Western industrialisation in both potential for mass production and material technologies. It is not a style per se, which can be identified via a catalogue of window shapes and swatches of colour, but rather starts with the contemplation of how space is being used and weighing up environmental factors for comfort and utility.

It is generally recognised that Modernist design was formally established in Europe in 1919 with the opening of the Bauhaus school of design in Germany. The school combined the disciplines of architecture, art and design, and its theories were exemplified in the work of innovators such as Walter Gropius, Mies van der Rohe and Le Corbusier. Frank Lloyd Wright, an American forerunner who derived much of his inspiration from the craftsmanship and principles of Japanese architecture, had a huge influence on these 'modern' practitioners in this early period. The philosophies of the Bauhaus evolved, peeling off across the globe and, with an increase in prosperity and technological advances after World War II, gained further traction. Eventually, these principles became the defining ethos for architects and designers worldwide from roughly 1940 to 1980, and for this reason the term 'Modernist' is married to 'Mid-Century'. It is worth noting that the terms 'modern', 'mid-century' and 'Mid-Century Modern' are not the same nor entirely interchangeable. To allay confusion and for the purposes of this book (though without strict academic rigour), the usage of the terms 'modern' and 'mid-century' pertain to the period (the mid-20th century) and what was culturally contemporary while living in that time, whereas 'Modernism' in its noun-y caps refers to the work informed by Modernist philosophers and design disciplines. 'Mid-Century Modern' is the Modernist work that was created during the mid-century period.

As Australia rode into the 20th century, there was no shortage of young people who took up Modernist ways of thinking, resulting in a multitude of career trajectories in architecture and design. Indeed, the narratives of our Mid-Century Modernist practitioners – unlike the narrow, expensive pathway of contemporary architectural study – bear out an astonishing variance. They include a Qantas pilot, Bill Baker; the grand final captain of an Australian Rules football team, Jack Clarke; an eyewitness to the Russian Revolution, Anatol Kagan; a member of one of Australia's most celebrated arts families, Robin Boyd; a self-taught ex-serviceman, Grant Featherston; and the studious protégé of Modernist titans Marcel Breuer and Oscar Niemeyer, Harry Seidler. Like most established Western histories, this tends to read as a roll call of white men, though that would be wilful erasure. As an acutely progressive movement, and thanks to the advancement of women from the 1930s in pursuits outside the home, the global Modernism vanguard involved many women architects and designers. In Australia, women plied their trade from the 1920s onwards in architecture firms, both as design leads and in successful partnerships with their husbands. Names like Mary Turner Shaw, Edith Emery, Eva Buhrich, Marion Hall Best, Mary Featherston and Helen Holgar dot the present discourse and deserve further exploration.

Amid all the residences attributed to famous names, there remain swathes of lovely Mid-Century Modernist Australian homes built by the 'journeymen' practitioners – the small-time architects, the engineers and the self-taught who are known only locally and often lost to anonymity. And though any building attached to a big name brings a certain level of innovation and prestige, Modernist tranquillity and charm can just as easily be found in the unassuming local example.

Modernist architectural philosophy is primarily governed by the environment in which the house is built, with deep consideration of conventions such as the sunlight and directional orientation, the existing vegetation and the movement of people within the house. It is concerned with the designation of spaces without simply building a warren of square rooms in which to plop furniture. The kitchen could be anywhere; the same for bathrooms – so where should they be positioned? Asking these questions and working on solutions for these matters may result in a dwelling where the front door does not face the street, and windows might be floor to ceiling or above head height, and not symmetrically aligned. Bathrooms might be hidden yet central (hooray for modern plumbing), while the living and dining rooms and kitchen are not cloistered from each other, separating the classes/sexes, but share a congenial space. Screens, split levels, benches or even a catwalk may separate or integrate certain quarters: sleeping, living, bathing.

Decoratively speaking, Victorian terraces tack on intricacies to promote the high-bred station of their owners: iron lacework, plaster ceiling roses, neoclassical fireplaces. These are augmented with chandeliers, carved-legged sofas and lace. By contrast, early Modernist expression in buildings and furnishings centres on simplifying form to the bare minimum and elevating the inherent traits of their materials – the grain of unpainted timber or marbling of stone, the texture of rough grass matting or natural cork, the sleekness of steel. Modernist designers, ever progressive, reached for the new, embracing materials including chrome tubing, coloured ceramics and large-scale glazing and techniques such as prefabricated construction and mass production.

Though Modernist principles seem like a given to us now, 100 years ago Modernist designers had to dismantle the Anglo-Saxon, childlike concept of a house in totality: the classic square with a triangle on top, and rectangular central door with a window on either side. Breaking societal concepts is not easy, and even today many housing developments still rely somewhat on this incredibly outdated, pre-Modernist template.

Mid-Century Modernism in Australia: A postscript

The promotion of Mid-Century Modernist concepts in Australian architecture began to wane around 1980. Instead of informing the design of houses and residential estates across the subsequent forty years, the philosophy was sidelined not only architecturally but also culturally. This may be attributed to underexplored factors including neoliberal capitalism, globalised manufacturing, a rising developer class and, particular to Australia, a regression to neo-colonial identity. Convict-heritage pride, Princess Diana and the approaching bicentennial celebrations of 1988 made a case for revisiting colonial aesthetics. The impact on our suburban landscape was dire, resulting in an infill of insipid lawn-lined streets and volume-built houses with no concern for insulation, orientation or indoor–outdoor relationship (though the appearance of the upsold 'al fresco dining area' did arrive by the 2000s). The ever-expanding footprint of houses devouring all green space reached its crescendo with the McMansion, a bloated statement of anti-design and consumerism.

In the 1980s and 90s the vanguard of Australian Mid-Century Modernist practitioners were ageing and, though a younger generation of architects evolved further to become celebrated visionaries executing one-off commissions for rarefied clients, much was lost in residential design for middle- and working-class Australia. Mid-Century Modernist buildings were ignored or derided as a 1970s key-party punchline and hit their nadir. Elegant mid-century residences and even entire suburbs to this day find themselves at the mercy of the 'wealth creator' class, who champ at the bit to knock them over and replace them with poor-quality townhouses or the aforementioned McMansions.

The very concept of Mid-Century Modern as a heritage designation has taken an overly long time to arrive. Fine Modernist architecture, the earliest examples of which are approaching 100 years old, is deserving of legal protection; however, recognition is glacially dawning on regulators. That said, a growing movement supporting the protection of more notable buildings and streetscapes is in motion. From the global DOCOMOMO to the local, such as Sydney Living Museums and the Robin Boyd Foundation, and to the grassroots like Beaumaris Modern, foot soldiers amass to extol the value of holding on to the Mid-Century Modernist buildings in our midst.

It is not all bad news. In this new century, the climate crisis in delivery mode and the renewed longing for the handcrafted and local is ushering in a comeback. Domestically there is no end to the list of impressive contemporary architects whose philosophies are founded in Modernism; every architecture firm noted in this book is a starting point. And in commercial practice, humanist ideals are finding new ascent with examples like Breathe's socially conscious and sustainable Nightingale Housing model, which began in Melbourne with The Commons (2013) and has now made its way to Adelaide, Sydney and Perth, as well as regional Australia. And so the beat goes on.

It's the vibe

Owing to its comeback in the past twenty years, the Mid-Century Modern 'style' has fallen prey to commodification and the usual misrepresentations in a market hungry for product. This includes entire industries of sweatshop furniture copied from old and young designers alike without due compensation or attribution, and online influencers declaring that a rather nondescript house slathered with white paint is somehow connected to Palm Springs. A lot of this is basic trend, a shallow commercial interpretation without the ephemeral, spiritual benefits that informed design can bestow on the human psyche. A surface treatment

might look cool for now, yet inherently does not ascribe to elemental principles and hence does not exude 'the feel'.

'It's the vibe' is a common refrain for those who inhabit well-designed spaces when they're asked to define what it is that sets these spaces apart. As a Western culture wholly concerned with the visual, this 'vibe' is tricky to translate into text, let alone to portray in images. You need to be in situ to truly experience it, and it may be felt as a pervading sense of tranquillity, the calmness that the careful modulation of light, air and sound can achieve. It allows movement through spaces that is intuitive and informal. This quality is harmonious yet so subconscious that it often captivates visitors before they know how to name it. Indeed, many a Mid-Century Modern householder initially takes on their home due to an intangible attraction; they like the way it feels, only afterwards falling down the rabbit hole of architectural revelation. This initial attraction, this vibe, cannot be achieved by a mere coat of paint or new flooring but is the result of inherent design ideals that encompass the consideration of the spaces for living, and working with natural elements in a resolution of physical and aesthetic balance.

Mid-Century Modernist furniture

It is reasonable to suggest that Mid-Century Modernism began and is perpetually rediscovered via furniture. The Bauhaus, after all, was an industrial design school. The desire to live in a Mid-Century Modern house is oft the endgame of a fantasy ignited by a Noguchi coffee table or West German vase collection. Most recently it was the slew of 1990s subcultures (think tiki bars and vintage cars) that propelled Mid-Century Modern and Scandinavian style into new ascent. The concurrent birth of the internet subsumed this cultural resurgence and pumped it with the new online economy. What was once the preserve of design tragics picking up a Featherston chair in a country op shop morphed into online marketplaces, dealers importing from Denmark and breathless name-dropping in design blogs.

Evolutionary too is the Mid-Century Modern aesthetic itself. Where once fine teak sideboards of the 1950s and 60s defined its appeal, a younger generation now covets the later lines of the 1970s and 80s: modular lounges, Cesca chairs (themselves a revival of Marcel Breuer's original design, circa 1928) and the injected plastic furniture of Guzzini, Kartell and our own Caroma.

The furniture design of postwar Australia embraced a scope of disciplinary hybridisation in which the same creative spirits that generated new shapes of furniture also plied their trade in lighting, interior design or fine art. Clement Meadmore began his career designing chairs and the interiors of Melbourne's Legend

Espresso and Milk Bar, and later established a notable reputation in public sculpture in the USA. Grant Featherston was a lighting designer before producing his most famous armchairs in the 1950s and 60s. These luminaries were joined by young businesses that became household names in Australia, among them Parker, Fler, Danish Deluxe and Tessa, which took inspiration from the unfussy, Scandinavian style of Modernism that married Modernist design with factory production techniques. Their pieces can still be found at Nanna's house and second-hand dealers aplenty.

Just as Mid-Century Modernist architecture has its icons of local and international fame running alongside the undocumented practitioners, so too does Mid-Century Modern furniture. For every dining table that carries a verified name, there are knock-offs. Here it can be said that not all knock-offs are equal, with some copies of the era utilising timbers and standards of craftsmanship now no longer a reality in today's mid-range furniture. The dispiriting demolition of irreplaceable Mid-Century Modern homes locally has also seen the criminal loss of custom-made joinery – bespoke pieces of unfathomable skill and irreplaceable timbers – and fabrics, though furniture dealers often rescue and resell these orphans when given the chance.

The Modernist Australian garden

The rise of Modernist architecture signalled the beginning of Australian maturity, one of transition from colonial outpost to a nation of unique character and richness, impacted by new arrivals and awakening to an understanding of the indigenous landscape and climate. In perfect parallel, the history of Australian gardening chronicles the same. The 19th-century tableaux of colonial homesteaders milling about a stifling English cottage in February heat is completed by the dogged watering of roses, the desiccated sticks lining the front yard. This ludicrous attempt to imprint English culture wholesale onto a landscape on the other side of the world began to fall away after World War I with the arrival of the progressive ideals articulated by Modernism in all its forms. And as the architecture and attitudes changed, so did the gardens.

Paradoxically, it is a recurring theme in Australian Modernism that it takes individuals new to Australia to recognise and extol the inherent beauty sitting right under our noses. American architect and landscape designer Walter Burley Griffin and his partner, fellow architect Marion Mahony Griffin, are examples of the 'influential outsider' in the early Modernist century. They were not only experimental in their architectural forays and civic planning but also in recognising and elevating Australia's

Patricia Callan

↑   Pelican House, also known as Myer
House (1956), in Mt Eliza, Victoria,
by Robin Boyd. The house is now
sadly demolished. Thankfully a
growing movement supporting the
protection of more notable buildings
and streetscapes is now in motion.
Photography: Mark Strizic. State
Library of Victoria Collection. sz201818.

Patricia Callan

natural environments. Arriving in Australia in 1913 with the commission to create the new capital of Canberra, the pair immediately took to bushwalking with like-minded locals and established architecture offices in Melbourne and Sydney. They designed new residential suburbs, including Castlecrag, the first ever to embrace the jagged Sydney bushland, and have been credited with the radical act of planting the lemon-scented gums – not oaks, not pines – that stand majestic 100 years later on the Swanston Street roundabout, next to colleges of the University of Melbourne. The seeds of indigenous botanica were sown into white Australia.

Around this time, Edna Walling, an English immigrant living in Melbourne, was on her way to becoming one of Australia's preeminent landscape designers. Seeking work with architects and eventually also developing her own housing subdivision, Walling toiled within the parameters of the Modernist feeder-style Arts and Crafts movement, which was linked to both the Griffins and Frank Lloyd Wright. Though harking back to the cottage gardens of her English upbringing, Walling's landscapes are infused with the romantic ramble of the wild and naturalistic. Pathways, nooks and low stone walls shrouded in overgrown greenery became her calling card, and from as early as the 1920s she utilised indigenous plants in her designs.

The serendipitous employment of a garden hand by Walling, an injured Gallipoli veteran by the name of Ellis Stones, was to be perhaps the most defining event in Australian landscape design. Stones worked steadfastly for Walling before moving into his own landscape design practice that extended upon her uninhibited vision by thoroughly incorporating the Australian bush. Rambling paths, rock placement, native flora and localised beauty were a constant. The guiding principles of Stones' philosophy – that 'nature is the greatest teacher' and 'gardens are for people' – echo those of Modernist architecture in their purpose and place within the earthly world. His concept of a courtyard as an essential green space for human engagement, especially within the confines of urban living, champions Modernist humanism over any strict visual propriety. In the same vein, the practical needs of the client remained paramount, including future changes in lifestyle.

Stones elevated landscape design to a formal discipline in Australian society. From the 1950s he pioneered the propagation of indigenous plants at his own nursery and passionately advocated their use. He abhorred town planners who clung to wildly inappropriate English garden conventions and the continued destruction of our bushland heritage on roadsides and in gardens and logging coupes. In the early 1970s he collaborated with Graeme Gunn and Merchant Builders to landscape the Winter Park Estate, one of the last Mid-Century Modernist forays into residential housing, where he planted the literal nuts and berries to complement the subdivision's architecture.

The best contemporary Australian landscape design, much like contemporary domestic architecture, germinated with these Modernist pioneers and now exponentially expands on these principles. A particularly revitalised energy of indigenous plant use and experimentation is visibly thriving in the examples in this book as well as all around us, right now. This evolution of naturalism and native plant adoption in Australian Mid-Century Modernist landscaping is our own country's tale to tell, but it is not the only form of Modernist garden design, then or now. As architecture speaks in dialects formed by place, time and fashion, so too do gardens. Take the austere minimalism of the gardens created in International Style in North America or Europe. Just as Western Modernist architecture drips with Japanese architectural convention, so too do these sweeping gardens, featuring clipped lawns, abstract bronzes, single charismatic trees and stone paths, reflect the mathematical elegance of Japanese landscaping.

In the 1940s, this formal European expression took a detour into the desert with the Mid-Century Modern landscapes of California. Particular to the southern hotspots – hello, Palm Springs – these designs signify the white man's awakening to the American West's timeless indigenous treasures: succulents, sandscapes, rocks and cacti. Throw into this fusion a Pacific palm tree and an inground pool for the likes of deified celebrities such as Frank Sinatra, and this landscape transmits a glamorous cachet that reverberates sixty years later. The Australian affection for a Palm Springs Modernist garden or elements thereof is understandable given the cultural impact of the American century, but it has grown substantially with the impacts of drought and the similarity of climate. A kindred botanical exchange is evident when viewing images of notable houses of the Californian Case Study House program, photographed by Julius Shulman under soaring eucalypts.

Renovating a Mid-Century
Modern Home

Patricia Callan

When you are surveying a Mid-Century Modern home with aspirations of renewal and renovation, navigating Mid-Century Modernist principles while also addressing all practical measures is a formidable starting point. For the entire lifespan of modernistaustralia.com I have been contacted with requests from across the country for details of skilled practitioners, trades and materials to help with such a journey. In the following section, my experiences in the renovation and extension of my family's architect-designed home appear alongside observations on this subject and serve to underline the professional skill and vision of the completed projects in this book. This is not a shopping list or an immutable 'how-to' guide as such, but rather a collection of themes, considerations and examples that may inspire and offer solutions for your own project, no matter the scale, budget or timeline.

Through my own Mid-Century Modern renovation and over years of seeking out and fervently advocating for such dwellings, I have discovered one overarching foundation to any successful project: a grounding of *integrity*. Integrity is *applied honesty*. Though each residence presented in this book is inherently different in age, scope and location, it is honesty to the original that underpins each home's unique cohesiveness and success. Without integrity, additions and changes are carried out apropos of nothing, with negligible relationship to the home's 'self'. This makes for discordant and unfit upgrades which never really work or which erase era-specific charisma.

To begin: Know thyself, know thine house

In the beginning there is provenance. Gather intelligence about the origin of the building. Start with the basics: Who designed this building? When was it built? Who commissioned it? Have there been changes over the years? The answers to these questions will surface formally and informally. Original owners and architects are the primary sources, along with contracts of sale and local government records. Old magazines and media may help. A professional heritage historian can be hired for a deep dive. The richest detail may be sourced from neighbours, especially elderly folk who have lived alongside the property for perhaps fifty years or more.

Origin information may lead to identifying a design and cultural category or era. This information is not accrued so you can commit to a slavish adherence to the original, aesthetically or otherwise, but rather to uphold a philosophy that any renovation to a building is best informed by a comprehensive 'reading' of it on every metric first. Know what you have before you change it, and understand why you are making that change – in other words, make any changes *intentional*.

The next evaluation is one of the self. Why did you, the owner, acquire this house in the first place? What do you love about it, and what needs to work better for you and others who'll live in it? Do you value having a smaller impact on Earth? Do you have a growing family to shelter? Do you garden, have hobbies or want to have guests stay over? This may seem rudimentary stuff, but when seeking to sympathetically update an existing home, every decision must be competently shaped for the utility of the owner.

Sometimes certain characteristics of Mid-Century Modern buildings are not compatible with contemporary needs but their retention addresses an owner's sentimental or aesthetic necessity. At our house, a 1970s concrete block home designed by Eoin Barnett, the low horizontal lines of the entry are anchored by a classic Modernist carport. Though we'd love a secure garage to lock up tools and bikes out of the sea air, we dismissed out of hand such an addition which, with its hefty concrete profile, would instantly turn our breezy home into a hostile fortress. In this vein, some owners may be happy to accommodate a smaller kitchen layout rather than risk losing the character of an adjoining dining space, while others still might buy a home in part for its thrilling butterfly roofline, even if that requires more attentive gutter clearing.

Renovation of a smaller-scale dwelling paradoxically presents a bigger undertaking, as it is often these residential projects that require the toughest decisions and most creative solutions due to tighter confines of budget and space. In these scenarios, it is all the more important to utilise all of the professional intelligence and creativity a budget will allow, to extract the most pleasing outcome.

Working with professional practitioners

Engaging professionals to transform a home can be a fraught exercise. Opening yourself up to potentially divergent personalities, predilections and vulnerabilities such as physical accessibility in conjunction with the expense of construction is not just a negotiation but an intimacy. As such, a compatible relationship between the client, architect, builder and/or interior designer exponentially increases the success of the final result. It pays to choose all help wisely and do the research beforehand. Budgetary constraints are always front and centre for anyone planning a renovation and cannot be brushed aside. That said, engaging a registered architect to manage a renovation or simply draw up a plan brings untold expertise, creativity and increased financial value to a home.

For our own renovation and a number in this book, such as Beachcomber House (see page 160) and Fender House (see page 242),

the first port of call was the original architect. We were grateful to consult with the architect of our home, Eion Barnett, regarding the design of our renovation. Who better qualified to advise on potential extensions and layouts embracing the inherent personality of the residence than the very mind which conceived the building in the first place? Access to original Mid-Century Modern architects in person, however, is a rare blessing, and aside from having historical documents at hand to guide you, a contemporary, sympathetic professional is the ideal.

When engaging an architect or designer, look at their prior work, talk to previous clients and find your groove with them on a philosophical level. Do they 'get' you? Do they appreciate your home as it stands now? What are their immediate thoughts and likes about the project? A common theme throughout the many projects in this book is trust. Clients often land on surprising ideas and ingenious solutions due to trusted relationships with their architects. A great practitioner will work with the building and clients, tailoring everything towards an excellent outcome for both, allowing you to see yourself and your living spaces through a multitude of possibilities.

Builders too require an understanding of a home's architectural history and intention; moreover, as tradespeople, they must deeply appreciate the qualities of materials and old craftsmanship in order to see a project through to its best. This is exceptionally important if carrying out the work without the project management of an architect, where the protection and retention of design and materials rest with the builder and the client.

A builder or other tradesperson who doesn't appreciate era-specific materials won't go out of their way to source the exact same material or a truly sympathetic equivalent if required, as did the mindful builders at GA House (see page 90) and Frankston House (see page 170), for example. The wrong tradesperson for your project may not understand how to work around in situ terrazzo or will argue against natural cork for a harder wearing white tile, a practical option yet an aesthetically diminishing one. Most importantly, a worthwhile builder working on a Mid-Century Modern renovation needs a heightened sensibility of the value of retention. The saving and reuse of building materials is environmentally sacrosanct but also financially and aesthetically essential in a country where so many historical homes of now-extinct materials and craftwork are simply tossed into a skip.

Mindfully addressing environmental matters

Concerns of ecological responsibility are a progressive and inherently Modernist ideal. With escalating industrialisation imperilling everything that binds us to Earth – wilderness, agriculture, biodiversity, and clean air and water – our own contribution to this situation becomes an urgent consideration. Curbing environmental impact has evolved exponentially in contemporary architecture and is based on a 'use less' mindset. This begins with the choice of demolition or renovation. Embodied energy (aka total energy use in just the construction of a home), as an example, can be more than 30 percent of a house's *entire energy use* over its fifty-year lifespan.[1] The energy rating system is one analytical way to measure the 'sustainability' of a building but is the act of knocking down a perfectly well-built house, throwing away all materials, and constructing a new 'seven-star rated' house truly 'sustainable' or ecologically conscious? Can retrofit resolve all issues of energy consumption and loss instead? How much can or should be salvaged? These deliberations are not specific to the houses shown here but the design ideals inherent in Modernism do lend extra impetus to ensuring that such matters are mindfully addressed from the outset and throughout each project.

Future thinking for insulation and energy

Australian housing stock has a deserved reputation for appalling thermal security. This includes early Modernist homes, many built during times of acute material shortage and rudimentary technology. The lack of insulation surety is forgiven for the early days. However, since the 1980s the wilful disregard of such matters by the building industry and regulators has seen the Australian home grow in every way yet remain as energy efficient as a tent. Natural thermal regulation for interior comfort was always a consideration in Mid-Century Modernism with regard to orientation and airflow, but now, in times of weather extremes and rising energy costs, it is a primary issue. Almost all projects presented here have undergone fundamental insulation, glazing, and heating and cooling system upgrades. In my experience of extending our home's footprint, the installation of premium wall and ceiling insulation as well as double glazing was essential. In addition to this, we duly replaced our old-school gas wall furnaces and hot water system with split systems and a heat pump in preparation for an incoming solar array to power them. These changes are now revealing themselves as an economic godsend within the present global gas market. Aside from the economic benefits, actively undertaking contemporary resolutions with regard to energy, soundproofing, climate and ambient comfort in the case of a Modernist home in essence elevates the original architect's intention.

Technology: On the periphery of consciousness

Technological utility is fundamental in most aspects of contemporary architectural practice, including renovation and retrofitting. The truth is, Mid-Century Modern houses were already a giant leap into the future in their innovative use of materials and fabrication. These advances occurred in conjunction with a cascade of unforeseen domestic improvements. Furthermore, these improvements were democratised, and accessible to a rising middle class, handing a majority of the population luxuries (primarily free time) previously only reserved for the ultra-wealthy. Developments included central heating, indoor plumbing and appliances such as electric wall ovens and dishwashers, the social implications of which, especially for women, are a topic for another book. Suffice it to say, the design and aesthetics of Mid-Century Modernist homes were born from a world encouraging of technological advancement. If Modernist icons such as Mies van der Rohe and Robin Boyd could witness the technology available today – from solar panels and wi-fi to 3D printing – they'd be leaping at the opportunity to utilise it. However, technology for technology's sake is not the intention; rather, it is always tempered by a human focus.

Updating new technology in a Mid-Century Modern renovation, though essential, must be duly considered for its purpose and placement. Ideally it will be utterly practical but not the focal point. Though many 'new' appliances of the mid-20th century aimed for a kind of integrated aesthetic – either in a crafted disguise, such as timber-encased televisions, or declaring a space-age futurism with white goods – today there is an unholy mishmash. The work of German designer Dieter Rams aside, a lot of domestic technology and appliances remain surprisingly ugly and visually discordant considering the literal position in the home these brands assume for their products. The half-baked 'designs' of planned obsolescence and profit-driven supply chains create objects and equipment that do no favours for anyone aesthetically. The trick is to devise clever and deeper integration, building, hiding and adjusting technology to be on the periphery of consciousness. None of the houses in this book feature equipment or machines front and centre. In each design approach this is a deliberate manoeuvre and often the culmination of a hard-won battle between spaces, objects and utility.

Identifying the nasties

The enthusiastic over-egging of technological discoveries in the 20th century and, moreover, the potential for limitless corporate profit gave rise to some insidious legacies. Asbestos and lead paint: can you name a more iconic duo in home renovation? Safety as a concept has developed exponentially over the years, and innovations are now subject to far more rigorous standards. No one wants to retain an old gas heater that, aside from poor efficiency, potentially pumps carbon monoxide into the living room. Degraded electrical wiring with no safety switch legally requires replacement. Poor drainage and exhaust systems propagate generations of mould. Oil heaters and briquette furnaces stand only as monuments to our doomed affair with fossil fuels. Each of these is a primary concern, first on the list to be dealt with in an effective and long-term resolution. Options for looking beyond the immediate with future-proofing should be explored in depth, such as the aforementioned replacement of gas with electricity connections or the installation of comprehensive guttering and water tanks, for extremities in rainfall.

Modernist domestic architecture is not without its archetypal issues. Flat rooflines built for their sleek visual impact can be a nightmare of choked box gutters causing terrible leaks, a conspiracy of wear, mediocre engineering and poor materials. Glazing of Mid-Century Modern homes, though extensive, can be of scant thickness, making for dramatic heat loss and higher energy use. Though common, like all repairs they are readily addressable, not insurmountable, and once corrected secure a home's future. Even dreaded asbestos, its use at its peak during the Mid-Century Modern construction period such that it infiltrates the majority of Australian housing stock, is just one more factor to carefully assess and then either leave undisturbed or have professionally removed. Good tradespeople with a long-term vision and consummate safety standards are invaluable in respect to reaffirming a safe and robust building, no matter what era.

Lighting: Balancing ambiance with utility

Australian light is like no other. It might require a trip to the northern hemisphere to truly understand the ultraviolet saturation levels in which we exist as concurrently brilliant and dangerous. In this new century, Australia's relationship with light in residential dwellings has shifted in a strange direction. Darkened spaces, perhaps fomenting bad memories of dank bedrooms and poor airflow, have been banished by an insatiable hunger for artificial light – piles of lights! – the brighter the better. Where once living rooms were perfunctorily serviced with a single fitting, an overabundance of downlights is now the norm. Spaces of relaxed togetherness, loungerooms and dining areas, are mindlessly fixed in a cool white intensity more suited to a laboratory. We have swung to the other extreme of the over-lit, perhaps without really understanding why. Like most decisions in renovation, the dissection of human use and wellbeing is key. Shadow and dark are design assets worth full consideration and application over thoughtless eradication.

Patricia Callan

↑   Technology is essential to our contemporary lives but requires deep design consideration to place it in the periphery of consciousness. Where is the tellie? Fisher House (see page 216). Photography: Sean Fennessy.

p. 22   The way we utilise living spaces demands that we address shadow and darkness as valid design choices over any boilerplate 'enhancement' via excessive lighting. GA House (see page 90). Photography: Sam Noonan.

Remember that Mid-Century Modernist architecture already prioritises natural light, with extensive glazing issuing the benefit of interiors that require negligible lighting during the daytime. Our own Modernist home only requires internal lights switched on at dusk or stormy days, such is the consideration for natural light in the original design, and a factor we deliberately continued throughout a newly built extension.

When making changes to any legacy residence, it is necessary to read the rooms in their original allure and find a balance between retaining this ambiance and improving contemporary utility. Practically speaking, it might call for like-for-like replacement of a beautiful vintage pendant or substituting a new, sympathetic local design. It may mean replacing a central, single outlet with two or three strategically angled downlights. For our home renovation, this lighting balance required that we address the original timber bulkhead lighting running throughout the dwelling. We retained this integral character feature but swapped out the flickering fluorescent tubes behind the timber pelmets for a warm LED strip to superb effect.

Contemporising old spaces with new lighting hardware is generally non-negotiable, if only for safety reasons, but it isn't something that can be simply resolved with the mindless installation of endless LEDs.

The power of light over our mood and interaction with others is so incredibly important yet desperately overlooked in everyday building. Light is a defining characteristic of our Australian lives. The quality of our artificial light, more than any other interior design choice, demands a variety of options and thoughtful consideration. When revisions are carried out successfully, it is a marker of a truly beautiful place to inhabit.

Updating the kitchen and bathrooms

Water, the life source which carves out canyons over millennia, certainly makes short-term work of even the most well-constructed bathroom or kitchen. Indeed, the first casualty in housing of a certain age is invariably the wet areas. (In otherwise all-original mid-century homes in any real estate listing, these spaces are commonly subject to a 1980s colonial or Bunnings flatpack update.) This is no one's fault in so far that heavy use and water take their toll, meaning these rooms simply require repair sooner than the rest of the home.

Cultural transformation similarly necessitates adjustments to the typically modest kitchen and bathroom configuration in the majority of Mid-Century Modern residences. Once simply grateful to have instant hot water and adequate drainage to supersede the gully trap, contemporary

Patricia Callan

Australia now demands expanded refrigeration, extra bathrooms and ever-larger island benches. Reimagining these places within the home and their more prominent role in family life can be potentially easier in Modernist residences, as the architecture always aimed to embrace this lifestyle anyway. Our own kitchen, hailing from 1979, was instantly attractive due to its large bench and all-timber cupboards, an open and beautiful space with the same resonance and scale as high-end bespoke builds today, despite its forty-year-old seniority and otherwise humble footprint.

All the homes in this book present an elegant array of devices and designs to address these tricky spaces. Solutions include moving a single dividing wall to extend an existing layout, as in House Kinder (see page 42); fidelity to era-expressive materials such as coloured tile and carpet through the application of a contemporary version, as in Lindfield House (see page 228); and the ingenious repositioning of original, nostalgic fittings such as basins and tapware, charmingly exemplified in Anglesea Cabin (see page 136). In our own bathroom refurbishment, new tile and timber replaced the degraded old and kept to the original neutral scheme, but we finished it with new orange tapware and flooring, boldly saluting the 1970s. A multitude of options in endless configurations can bring beautifully cohesive and joyful practicality to these hard-worn spaces.

Furnishing with honesty to self

In Mid-Century Modern decor – the textile design, carpet, tile and wallpaper – the overarching signature is bold colour and pattern. Optimistic and unbowed, decor design of the 1940s through to the 1970s catalogued successive experiments of daring and flair. This progression is revealed in the abstracted pastels and Western-appropriated 'primitive' graphics of the 1950s moving into the bolder Op Art geometry, plastic and metallic luxe of the 1960s, then taken downtempo to the homespun weave and crunch of the 1970s.

When furnishing a renovated Modernist home, the acquisition (and possible refurbishment) of second-hand furniture, textiles and the like carries noble benefits in environmental impact, reducing costs and preserving materials and craftsmanship. Alternatively, purchasing locally made and manufactured contemporary furniture – conceivably future icons – is a worthy investment because it supports good designers at the grassroots.

Whichever direction interior tastes extend, the key to success is, once again, honesty to self, achieved by honouring your personal affections, style and heirlooms. Every household is the physical expression of memories, style and aspiration, forming individual places of comfort and our very concept of home. Each residence showcased in this book, and every owner therein, expresses an inherent love of Mid-Century Modern design and possesses items from that era, yet they are combined with pieces from other periods and places in a perfect entirety. Wild and colourful or minimal and monotone and everything in between, the character and beauty of an interior space can be created using the furniture, textures and design forms of any decade in potentially limitless variations.

Gardening: Balancing principles, context and desires

Applying Modernist principles to a garden, as with buildings, depends on the character of the property and your needs. There is little value in creating a show-stopping garden that doesn't hold emotional resonance for you or is impractical to maintain. At the other end of the spectrum are endless lovely houses across the country blighted by garden-as-afterthought, a veritable sea of neglected rockeries, plopped-in yukkas and insipid lawn. A garden guided by Modernist principles can be simple, requiring minimal maintenance, or endlessly experimental and labour intensive, but in any situation, just like the renovation of a Mid-Century Modernist home, deliberate decision-making focused around familiar principles is key.

First it is vital that you consider your own personal desires for your garden or landscape. What plants do you like? Do you want a cool oasis? A productive vegetable patch? A bushland refuge, or something that borrows from each? In keeping with the intentional foundation of garden creation, it is best to pinpoint what you want and then build it from there. Drawing on the creativity of a professional landscape designer to help you answer these questions can be invaluable. A trained garden designer, like an architect, can distil personal tastes and then offer incredible botanical knowledge and design solutions, especially for more utilitarian spaces such as courtyards, pool sides and the links between, successfully transforming your outdoor world into a cohesive whole. The results of a dedicated garden designer forging a harmonious extension of the architecture can be seen in the sublime landscape of the Western Australian City Beach House (see page 182) and an alternative Victorian response at Fisher House (see page 216).

A clear cognisance of Australian climates and understanding (via experimentation or expertise) of what will thrive is foundational knowledge for the creation of any contemporary garden. The pioneering legacy of Ellis Stones is evident in many of this book's projects in the application of local plants that flourish and bring textural interest as well as the benefit of insects and birds to the landscape. The ever-expanding variety and nifty use of native plants in partnership with other suitable vegetation also makes for less maintenance and resource use in the long run. House Kinder (see page 42) harnesses this to great effect with the adoption of local, self-sufficient coastal elements – succulents, grasses and sand – eradicating the pointless lawn nature strip in the process. The specific placement of plants (especially trees) to address climatic issues is another signpost of Modernist environmental cognisance. A classic example is to plant a deciduous tree by a northern window to allow sunlight to enter the house during the cooler months but shield it from the harsh Australian summer sun.

Time plays an intrinsic role in landscapes and gardening. A prominent tree, for example, is twenty-plus years in the making, with its long maturation exponentially increasing its benefit and beauty to all. But exactly like Mid-Century Modern buildings, the retention of large trees on private land is increasingly fraught, with subdivision taking precedence over character and ecological concerns. Keeping a magnificent tree or, for that matter, a rocky outcrop or stand of grasses, provides an ideal focal point and structure from which the rest of the design environs can be extended. At the Quarter Deck (see page 100), for instance, the house is made all the more majestic by the soaring gums that surround it, retained to frame the sparkling water view.

Salvaging and relocating otherwise discarded plants is an incredibly economic and savvy way to expand a garden and similarly bolster character. At GA House (see page 90), the heroic rescue of a mature frangipani tree turned a botanic beauty destined for landfill into the sculptural centrepiece of the front yard.

The future they deserve

Achieving a sympathetic renovation with all the practical, emotional and philosophical ideals that entails is not a simple task, and it's important to realise that we won't always pull it off in some absolutist vision of perfection. However, the more we appreciate and seek to understand Australia's Mid-Century Modernist residences and their makers, the better equipped we are to treat them with integrity, and ultimately the more successful we will be in ensuring these precious dwellings attain the future they deserve.

1   T Weterings and J Tustin, 'Energy Consumption Benchmarks: Electricity and gas for residential customers', ACIL Allen Consulting, Melbourne, Victoria, 13 October 2017.

What Does Mid-Century
Modern Look Like in Australia?

Patricia Callan

To discuss Australian Mid-Century Modernist design is to grapple with contradiction. The contradiction is born of this architecture as a living *set of values*, rather than some immutable style. And like any living cultural exchange, such as music or filmmaking, the course of 100 years and immersion across the globe breeds schools and styles that adopt local cultural affectations and climatic necessities, and bend to fashion and technology across time.

Within Australian Modernism, there is a constant lineage of individual homes, conceived by architects known or unknown to us now, that were designed with Modernist principles using era-specific materials and that, in their creative selves, warrant no further labelling. That said, there are common 'variants' worth identifying. The following is an utterly unacademic summary of recognisable versions of Australian Mid-Century Modernist residential architecture.

← Domain Park Flats (1959–62) in South Yarra, Victoria, by Robin Boyd. Photography: Mark Strizic. State Library of Victoria Collection. sz201952.

What Does Mid-Century Modern Look Like in Australia?

1930s Onwards: European Émigré

From the 1930s onwards, a diaspora of European creatives fled annihilation across Europe. Departing the cosmopolitan centres of Berlin, Prague and Budapest, they made Australia, then a colonial backwater, their future. These educated professionals introduced a sophistication of intellect and creativity to a fledgling nation ripe for something other than the prevailing British custom. For Modernism in Australia, it was a game-changer. Throughout their careers these European architects and designers explored individual aesthetics and achieved different levels of success but the prevailing doctrine was Modernist. Legendary names such as Harry Seidler, Frederick Romberg, Iwan Iwanoff and a hundred others punctuate our architectural and design discourse to this day.

European Émigré

1910   1920   1930   1940

World War I–1930s: Early Modern and Inter-War

The beginnings of Modernism in Australia, dating from World War I up to the late 1930s, include the Arts and Crafts movement as propelled by Frank Lloyd Wright. Later buildings in this period embody the sleek glamour of Art Deco or Moderne and sister variant P&O Style, replicating the heft and luxury of modern shipping liners. In addition to this, built forays into 'alternative' estates arose, driven by architects, with a focus on communal living and natural environs. Notable examples include Fishwick House by Walter Burley Griffin and Marion Mahony Griffin (Castlecrag, 1929); Cairo Flats by Acheson Best Overend (Fitzroy, 1936); Wyldefel Gardens by WA Crowle and John Brogan (Potts Point, 1936); and Prevost House by Sydney Archer (Bellevue Hill, 1937).

Early Modern and Inter-War

Post-War Project Housing

1940s–70s: Post-War Project Housing

Though with pre-war roots, the concept of pre-designed houses began in earnest with the end of World War II and the civic necessity to house an influx of immigrants and a boom of young families. A parade of Australia's most formative Mid-Century Modern architects directed and produced designs (purchased over the counter by the general public) expressly for housing schemes collectively referred to as 'Project Plan'. Though not individually site-specific, these plans offered new Modernist approaches in construction and design never before experienced. They promoted steel-frame fabrication, floor-to-ceiling windows, open plan kitchen and living spaces, inbuilt appliances and heating and cooling technology. Notable examples include the Beaufort Home by Arthur Baldwinson (1946); *The Age* Small Homes Service (1947–70s, initially headed by Robin Boyd); Victa Homes (1950s–60s); Lend Lease (1960s, Nino Sydney); Pettit + Sevitt (1961–70s, Ken Woolley and Michael Dysart); Merchant Builders (1965–80s); and Winter Park Estate (1970s, Graeme Gunn).

Patricia Callan

1950s–60s: The Fibro Beach House

A unique expression of functionality and era, the Australian mid-century beach house remains unclassified as a Modernist subset. It arose postwar when new-found middle-class prosperity enabled the luxury of summer holidays, yet reflected the humble living standards and material shortages of those times. The beach houses were mostly constructed by their owners in the 1950s and 1960s from cheap, available materials. Their claim to Mid-Century Modernism lies in the conventions of the contemporaneous design of project plan homes: small yet serviceable spaces with flat or skillion rooflines, and open plan cooking, dining and living areas. Painted in optimistic hues of baby blues, mints, yellows and pinks, they remain the first and only instance of Australians ever employing a veritable rainbow of external house colours. Not signposted on any historical heritage records, nor part of any local architecture walking tours, these remnant houses can still be found in established holiday spots along all coastlines of the country.

The Fibro Beach House

Brutalism

1950s–70s: Brutalism

So named from the French *béton brut* (raw concrete), this later architectural variation dating from the 1950s to 1970s is at once fiercely loved and derided. Monumental in its unadorned pre-cast forms, Brutalist architecture also carries connotations of totalitarianism, as a visual assignation of communist Cold War states, though it is most commonly seen in Australia in the institutional context of universities, public pools and council offices. Residentially, Australian brutalism may be most famously exemplified in the Sirius building by Tao Gofers, designed for the Housing Commission of New South Wales (Sydney, 1979). Dominating the landscape and primitively gorgeous when partnered, in the South American tradition, with lush plant life, Brutalist buildings are a polarising presence – recent years have seen, sadly, many thrilling examples demolished. Perhaps now the time is ripe for a reappraisal.

1950   1960   1970   1980

1950s Onwards: Sydney School

From the mid-1950s a rising cohort of Sydney-based architects delved into ideas of a particularly naturalist Modernism. Taking cues from the American model of Frank Lloyd Wright's organic Prairie School, these architects designed and constructed houses that were cast as one with the bushland environment. The collective output of this group of architects is referred to as the Sydney School (naturally, most of the architects so associated don't recognise the term at all). These homes were built with a purist eye for Australia's wild environs and incorporate rough-hewn, brown-stained timbers and stone, rustic ceramic tile and unadorned exposed brickwork with minimal paint. Internally they can be complex, with split levels, stairs and living spaces laid out in all directions. Notable examples include Audette House by Peter Muller (Castlecrag, 1953); Jack House by Russell Jack (Wahroonga, 1957); Rickard House II by Bruce Rickard (Turramurra, 1962); and Baudish House by Ken Woolley (Sydney, 1964).

1960s–70s: Public Housing Towers

This is perhaps the most maligned version of Modernism in Australia, and one that culture warriors love to point out as the dystopian manifestation of (shock horror) *socialist ideals*. Though these apartment blocks assume various guises from the 1940s onwards, it is the 1960s Housing Commission towers of sparse, International Style architecture that garner the most attention. These apartment complexes, with their children's playgrounds and shared laundries, remain in their inner-urban locations and speak to the societal effort to decamp the city's impoverished families from Depression-era slums. Each Housing Commission flat held the optimism of offering a private sanctuary within a larger, vibrant community for society's most vulnerable, though they were perhaps less successful in practise than theory and now stand tired following sixty years of wear and tear. Examples of such towers are found in historically disdained but now desirable city hotspots such as Melbourne's Albert Park (Victoria Avenue) and Fitzroy (Napier Street); and Sydney's Redfern (Morehead Street).

Sydney School

Public Housing Towers

What Does Mid-Century Modern Look Like in Australia?

The following pages celebrate homes from across Australia that have been renovated, refurbished and modified for contemporary living, completed with the utmost care and integrity. These dwellings reverberate with the character and attributes of the Mid-Century Modernist ideals and materials behind their original conception. The personalities and requirements of their custodian owners are expertly woven through each project, standing as a singular testament to the creativity and toil of the architects, designers, builders and landscapers tasked with each contemporary update. You are invited to view these homes as a source of inspiration, a vacation, a destination, an education – the choice is yours.

New Modernist Houses

Location	Kew, Victoria
	Wurundjeri Woi Wurrung Country
Original architect	Anatol Kagan
Renovation date	2019
Renovation architect	Kennedy Nolan
Renovation builder	Weiss Builders
Interior design	Kennedy Nolan
Landscape design	Owners
Photography	Derek Swalwell

1953

Kagan House

Anatol Kagan–Kennedy Nolan

The river bends of Kew's Studley Park are lined with many of the suburb's mansions and close to its private schools. Intriguingly, through the postwar days of the late 1940s, an incredibly progressive cohort coalesced in the subdivided slopes of this genteel suburb. Hosting soirées for artisans of high bohemia, these monied patrons bought paintings, supported theatres and asked emerging Modernist architects to design their homes. As such, Kew stands as a preeminent mecca of remarkable Mid-Century Modernist homes, a place where, unlike most of the country, these architectural examples have remained relatively secure.

Within that micro-history, this residence was the first domestic house commission for a young émigré architect, Anatol Kagan, for David and Florence Bell. Kagan would go on to local acclaim with many notable buildings to his name, dotting the north and south sides of the Yarra River. Original plans for this two-bedroom residence date back to 1950, though it was not completed until 1953, which can be attributed to material rationing of the day. In original photographs it appears, newly constructed, sitting in a bare paddock.

The house stood, thankfully, intact and cared for over the successive decades while the re-established bushland matured around it into soaring gums over sun-dappled culs-de-sac. Eventually, the long-term owners resolved to renovate. They settled on local firm Kennedy Nolan to helm the project, setting in motion the transformation of this already fine slice of Mid-Century Modern legacy into something far more practical and exuberant.

Ever mindful of the era's design principles and creative impetus, the architects' first stop was a grounding in Kagan's biography, written by architectural historian gun-for-hire Simon Reeves. Next, they undertook a thorough strip-back, assessment and tweaking of the internal layout to resolve its eccentricities and inefficiencies. A thorough update for contemporary amenities and movement underlined their brief, along with a request for extra accommodation for intergenerational living. The latter was neatly addressed by excavating and renovating the subfloor garaging space. These understorey works ensured the house expanded on practicality while maintaining its singular, historical form.

Opening the house to the north-facing backyard, another aspect unexplored by Kagan, required considerable problem-solving in regard to pool fencing and establishing links to the rest of the home and presented as additionally challenging upon execution, due to the slope of the block. However, the brilliant professional conceptualisation ultimately transfigured this formerly dead zone into an entirely new and connected space for social fun-times and relaxation. A similar extension of social place-making was replicated at the front with an expansion of the deck.

Deciding on a visual character, including a material palette, the architects drew upon the culture of 1950s Melbourne, particularly its nightclubs and its milk bars, with softened pine green and triangular supergraphics as standouts. All parties shared a desire to ensure the era-specific integrity, one of extreme austerity, leading to reimagined material choices such as the kitchen pegboard and chequer pattern of the tiles in a delightfully nostalgic twist. Externally, the masonry had been diluted to a hodgepodge of surfaces and hence rough-cut render along with crazy paving and sectional elevation of the cream brick was employed to return the building to a cohesive whole and texturally ground it within the gorgeous native landscaping.

Ultimately, through their steadfast appreciation of their charge and thoughtful engagement of considered professionals, the owners took a building of architectural legacy from the edge of practical obsolescence and turned it into a landmark of jubilant wonder.

Anatol Kagan–Kennedy Nolan

↑　Connecting the house with outdoor living spaces including an expanded front deck and backyard pool was paramount in the new works, reflected internally by this nook with a view.

←　The architects resolved inefficiencies in the original floor plan, opening it up for more intuitive movement between living spaces.

← Contemporary furniture and fittings throughout the house – here in a bedroom – embody the spirit of Modernist design. Kitty approves.

→ The material palette deliberately references the limitations of early 1950s austerity with a creative twist, including the use of pegboard in the kitchen.

Anatol Kagan–Kennedy Nolan

Anatol Kagan–Kennedy Nolan

↑   A set of Featherston 'Scape' dining chairs, loyal to the colour scheme of black and deep teal, peep from the dining room.

←   The fireplace is retained in its original form but augmented by luxe furnishings, artwork and gossamer drapery that filters the natural light.

→   Defining one edge of the lounge, a solid white stair-rail featuring a pattern of triangles in relief repeats the pine green supergraphics found externally.

← Disparate external wall textures are brought together via strategic rough-cut render, painted sections and cream brick.

→ The retro milk bar–inspired graphics hit all the right notes in a playful new pool area.

Anatol Kagan–Kennedy Nolan

Kagan House

Location	Beaumaris, Victoria
	Boonwurrung Country
Original architect	Unknown
Renovation date	2021
Renovation architect	Wilko Architecture
Renovation builder	Owner–builder
Interior design	Wilko Architecture
Landscape design	Wilko Architecture
Photography	Derek Swalwell

1954

House
Kinder

Unknown-Wilko Architecture

p. 42   This house was being marketed for its land value only when it was purchased by a German-born architect, newly arrived in Australia, and his partner. They spent the next four years transforming it into this elegant family home.

p. 43   The beachside environs and remnant ti-tree informed the new landscaping of crushed rock, succulents and grasses.

←   A 1970s-era dark brick wall dominating the main living space was treated with linear repointing and light concrete render to draw it closer to the 1950s cream brick of the original.

In 2014, Wilko Doehring, an architect born and trained in Germany and working in the Australian office of John Wardle, was looking to settle down in Melbourne with his partner. After they'd fruitlessly trawled bayside real estate for some time, an agent suggested a lingering 'piece of land' they might like to look over. They soon discovered not just land but a dilapidated house, dejected and ignored. The sales material spruiked dimensions and square metreage, a familiar death knell for many modest postwar homes. Upon inspection, they explored a wreck of broken windows, leaf-strewn vanities and termite-afflicted timber. The main living spaces were subject to the heavy dank of a 1970s medieval-themed do-over with all the gloomy brickwork and wrought iron fittings that implies.

However, Wilko, who possesses a scholarly appreciation for Modernist architecture, saw through this detritus and recognised the building's qualities as a valid starting point for a new family home. The identity of the original architect remains elusive, but documentation revealed that the house was constructed in 1954 by a local builder called Kinder, an appealing coincidence for the family-focused couple. It still held architectural elements worthy of advancement, including expanses of timber-framed windows and total northern orientation. The architect knew that some interior tweaking could enhance the flow of daily living and entertaining, without the need to extend the footprint of the building.

'Eating the elephant one bite at a time', as Wilko describes it, they commenced four years of renovation grind. He applied his forensic knowledge and European sensibilities of thermal expenditure – a field embarrassingly underdeveloped in Australian housing – to addressing the climatic aspects. Wilko eschewed the go-to of installing double-glazed windows for temperature modulation, instead opting for a comprehensive plan of air-sealing in conjunction with massive measures of insulation.

Seemingly endless weekends saw the owners repair and rebuild the windows, the stripped layers of paint revealing decades of prior colour choices. The inherent natural beauty of the original timber was celebrated by repurposing all salvageable lengths in a feature wall in the entry and hallway. The sun-filled entry deliberately divides the living from the sleeping wing, and Wilko theorises this was an architectural 'grand gesture' added to make a humble home feel all the more expansive – which it does to great effect.

In the dining room, a mix of pale concrete render and ingenious repointing resolved the 1970s brickwork. By removing the incongruous mission brown and deep grout lines, the central space reverted to lightness and cohesive harmony with the original 1950s fair brick. A load-bearing wall dividing the original kitchen and dining section was removed to fulfil the family's need for a larger, workable kitchen and extra storage. The large island bench, a horizontal companion to the dining table and floating hearth which share the space, was built in its place as an intuitive gathering post for friends and family. Similarly, the concrete patios extending out from the living areas were reappointed in natural timber, these outdoor spaces embracing the sun's path and enabling easy indoor–outdoor movement for summer dinners and children's play on the enclosed lawn.

Once the garden's magical ti-trees were released from their weeds, they revealed their sculptural magnetism, providing a natural screen from the road. Further landscaping involved replacing the insipid, water-thirsty lawn 'nature strip' with a beach pathway built from literal tonnes of gleaned stone tailings, festooned with locally indigenous grasses and saltbush.

Perhaps the most startlingly lovely quality of this residence is the cream brick exterior, still ubiquitous to the Australian suburban landscape yet maligned and, sadly, in the past twenty years, unforgivably rendered and/or painted over by any amount of home 'improvement' projects. Here it is reborn clean and untouched, its golden brilliance framed by white timber windows and eaves, evoking pure summer nostalgia. As per the now classic trope of the Australian Modernist story, it takes a relative newcomer to remind us of our local beauty in plain sight and elevate it to worthy re-appreciation.

House Kinder

← When too much storage is never enough: the owner–architect utilised every available inch in the kitchen for neat packing away, including file drawers installed above head height.

→ A dividing wall between the modest kitchen and dining area was removed and a new island bench built to open up the existing space and create a central locus for socialising.

House Kinder

↑ The owners were adamant that
the house could be reborn as a
beautiful and completely liveable home,
without expanding on the existing
1954 footprint.

↘ The central bathroom has been
transformed into a functional family
space of super-insulated cosiness.

→ The modestly sized bedrooms, like
the rest of the home, are elegant and
exacting in the use of every available
space, including the creation of this
delightful study nook in the guest room.

House Kinder

→ The cream brick exterior, so often subject to denigration under thick renders and paint in contemporary renovations, has here been allowed to stand proud in its golden Mid-Century Modern brilliance, framed by windows and eaves detailed in white.

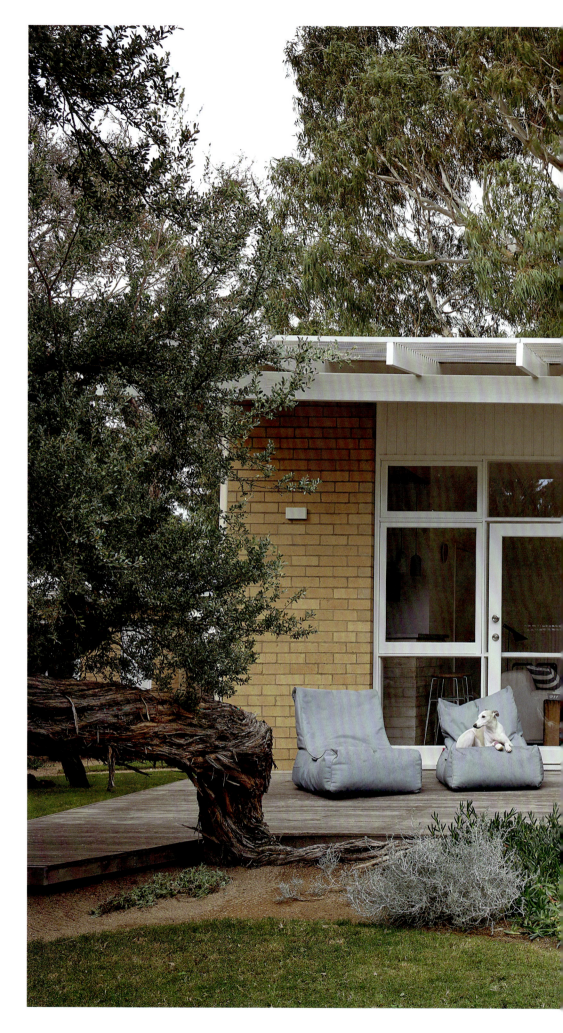

Unknown–Wilko Architecture

House Kinder

Caulfield
Townhouse

1956

Location	Caulfield North, Victoria
	Boonwurrung Country
Original architect	Unknown
Renovation date	2011
Renovation builder	Owner–builder
Interior design	Norwood Designs, owner
Photography	Tim Shaw

54

p. 52 A local landmark, this complex of two townhouses remains a stunning reminder of the rich creative heritage bestowed on Australia by its mid-century European diaspora.

p. 53 Sunlight beams through the windows of the chic stairwell, completed in palladiana paving and with a shapely metal balustrade.

← An enduring theme within this book is that each project is as contemporary and as individual as its present owners – there are no retro museums or shrines to long-dead architects. Each home reflects an individual personality at its heart.

The suburb of Caulfield North, indeed the entire slice of south-eastern Melbourne in which it sits, reverberates with a richness of a particularly Eastern European flavour. This townhouse comprises the top half in a complex of two that is a local landmark. An example of this distinct postwar émigré character in its design and detailing, it was inhabited by a succession of Jewish European owners for its first fifty years. Its architect is unknown, and the clues to its age lie in the Olympic ring motifs set into the windows and the green and gold balcony panelling – these hint at the 1956 Melbourne Olympics, and perhaps a cultural embrace by new arrivals of their fledgling city, which at that point was tentatively making its world-stage debut.

The Modernist architectural emphasis on light and airflow integrates with genteel 1950s elegance in this three-bedroom, two-bath residence and attracted Rod Duke of Norwood Designs, who purchased it in 2011. Though the townhouse was a little run-down at the time, the new owner relished its generous proportions and clean International Style metal windows and balconies, which he says make for 'the most amazing light show, from the early morning east to the hues of sunsets in the west'. Also attractive was the character found in coloured and etched glass panes and the palladiana marble stairwell with its shapely, metal balustrading. The rich abundance of finely crafted detail speaks to a progressive, European mindset of the mid-century that regarded townhouses as a fitting, even glamorous housing option for an entire lifetime, not merely, as we often see today, a shoddily constructed investment opportunity for self-styled developers.

Utilising his own skillset and eye for design, the owner immediately set to work on a renovation that would marry contemporary elements with an elevation of the building's Mid-Century Modern style and a nod to distinct local heritage. As always, the foundation repair work was first, involving a thorough strip-back of the 1980s-renovated kitchen and bathroom, as well as rewiring, plumbing and, most importantly in higher density living, bolstered soundproofing.

Ensuring fidelity to the era while updating for today within a strict footprint required a combination of interior design methods. In some instances, simply replacing old with new was best, as was the case for the cork flooring. In others, the adoption of existing motifs dictated the design approach; the triangular etchings in the glass doors and the geometric balconies of the neighbourhood are templates for the kitchen joinery, bench legs and loungeroom shelving. Elsewhere the owners opted for a dial-up of 1950s Hollywood drama, as seen in the bathroom with its wild step-up bath and bold mosaic tiles.

In addition to new joinery, the owners remodelled the kitchen to make it a spacious, social centre, gathered around a bespoke 4-metre island bench. Clever yet hidden technology was installed, which Rod describes as 'integrated appliances, pull-out shelving, Hafele trickery'. Employing surreptitious technology in historic residences is an astute measure to protect the ambiance of timelessness, without compromising on the vastly improved ease of contemporary amenities.

Accompanying this renovation is the owner's collection of furniture, art and lighting pieces, which creates idiosyncratic spaces of occasional depth and symbolism, such as in the bedrooms, and shields the residence from becoming a museum scene of strictly Mid-Century Modern performance. Instead, it presents as a collection of individual items, traversing a range of eras and holding personal meanings and an inherent design quality. An acknowledgement of self and personal styling in this way imbues any home with honesty, and in this case makes for a stunning outcome, one that celebrates history and design, without being a slave to any of it.

Caulfield Townhouse

→ The owners were first drawn to
the home's incredible natural light,
a benefit of these expansive and sleek
International Style metal windows.

Caulfield Townhouse

← Late-night revelry is facilitated by the new 4-metre island bench in the refurbished kitchen, its re-laid cork flooring a nice homecoming for this era-specific material.

→ The triangular motif in bespoke cabinetry, shelving and bench legs is a salute to the geometric etchings on its original glass entry doors and the balcony metalwork of other local Mid-Century Modern apartment buildings.

←   The drama is dialled up in the bathroom with bright colours and a step-up bathing 'altar' fit for a Hollywood starlet.

→   Small mosaic tiles and laminate, ubiquitous in so many mid-century bathrooms, is reinstated here in a minimal yet alluring confluence of the now and then.

Caulfield Townhouse

Unknown-Norwood Designs

↑ Since this wave of Mid-Century Modern, European-style complexes, Australian high-density residential buildings have never maintained such liveable form en masse, with most contemporary, affordable apartments poorly designed, lit and insulated.

← A darker treatment creating a restful space and stunning original parquetry – such a rarity these days – evoke a distinctly European sensibility in this bedroom.

　　Caulfield Townhouse

Location	Avalon Beach, New South Wales
	Garigal Country
Original architect	Loyal Alexander
Renovation date	2010–22
Renovation architect	Trace Architects
Renovation builder	Graeme Bell, owner–builder
Interior design	Trace Architects
Landscape design	Graeme Bell, owner–builder
Photography	Simon Whitbread

1957

Alexander House

Loyal Alexander – Trace Architects

p. 64   Alexander House was painfully run-down when purchased by the current owners; it took them twelve years of strategic toil to return the home to the stunning celebration of style it is today.

p. 65   A timber plant stand and retro arc lamp are just two of many Mid-Century Modern pieces perfectly at home in this house.

←   Walls of windows line the main living and dining spaces, bringing the outside in and promoting an active commune with nature.

In the aftermath of the Global Financial Crisis, with Sydney's professional class and their finances in flux, a previously unknown standout of Mid-Century Modernist style snuck onto the market. Jaw-dropping in form and potential, this dilapidated residence was summarily overlooked by agents, who instead spruiked its 1400 square metres of land as a 'development opportunity'. Architect Graeme Bell of Trace Architects and his partner, fresh off the back of a Federation-era house renovation, leapt upon the transaction as a new family home and project. History repeats, as this residence had been originally designed and built by a local architect, the mysterious Loyal Alexander, as his own family residence.

With an affinity for the era and an optimistic mindset, the owners' task of peeling back years of neglect and earlier additions took off slowly. They adopted a philosophy of a room-by-room refurbishment which, though allowing the family to live within the home for the duration and manage finances, required a Tetris-esque strategy for life, work and movement, the commencement of certain works reliant on the completion of others. This concentrated approach resulted in an immense twelve-year effort from start to finish, a temporal indicator of a true labour of love.

Clearing the inaccessible driveway was just one of the first jobs at the residence, which on first glance seemed in fair condition but ended up needing far more toil than initially anticipated: an old, familiar tune. The striking butterfly roof, for example, though now fully repaired with a wide gutter capacity and easy cleaning access, had presented as a holey mess. Graeme recalls that during the first few years the existing 'leak-proofing system' comprised a ceiling-glued plastic funnel, internal pipes and a bucket to be emptied during storms. The kitchen, now elegant in two-tone joinery, was likewise a progressive effort, installed in three sections, at three different intervals.

To select the interior palette and fittings Graeme leant into his architectural practice, which seeks materials attuned to the specific genre of a residential project. For his own home, this started with research and the eBay procurement of the August 1958 *House & Garden* magazine that featured the home as a standout example of the new modern living. The article pictured the internal rainbow of pinks, oranges and blues of high 1950s domesticity, hints of which revealed themselves here and there in the removal of old paint and additions.

This original kaleidoscope understood, the owners instead opted to pursue more contemporary neutrality so next contacted the curators of Harry Seidler's 1950 Rose Seidler House, across town in Wahroonga, to confirm the exact white used in that similarly bush-set Modernist monument. They then applied this shade throughout the majority of the residence, allowing for accents of era-specific flourish including the elegant timber joinery, the pastel bathroom tile, the terrazzo and the canary-gold front door. Refurbishment to celebrate integral features like the stone fireplace and breeze blocks of the lower facade was augmented with a considerable collection of Mid-Century Modern furniture and personal artifacts, all evolving into a dazzling whole.

After more than a decade of steadfast toil, this home, which in another timespace was summarily bulldozed, now is a celebrity. The site of films and photoshoots and the subject of its own social media pages, it stands as a testament to the labour, creativity and unrelenting optimism of its owners. It is a true landmark of its time, whose time has come around again, in triumph.

Loyal Alexander–Trace Architects

↑   Mid-Century Modern domestica is typified in these delightful pastel canisters.

←   Popping with glorious 1950s-style two-tone joinery, the kitchen was refurbished in three separate sections at three different stages of the renovation.

← Modernism holds fast to the inherent qualities of the materials pictured here – in the shiny metallic pendant light, fibrous wall art, timber and fur.

↙ Two-tone joinery is part of a new built-in wall unit housing shells, books, art and bugs.

↓ Talismans of the natural world – animal, vegetable and mineral – find display spots everywhere.

→ Art and furniture with Modernist influences invite engagement through their informal positioning.

Alexander House

← Floor-to-ceiling glazing floods the dining space with air and light, while timber flooring offers warmth underfoot.

→ Mosaic tiles and terrazzo have made a welcome comeback in the world of renovation, and are particularly appropriate to Mid-Century Modern refurbishments.

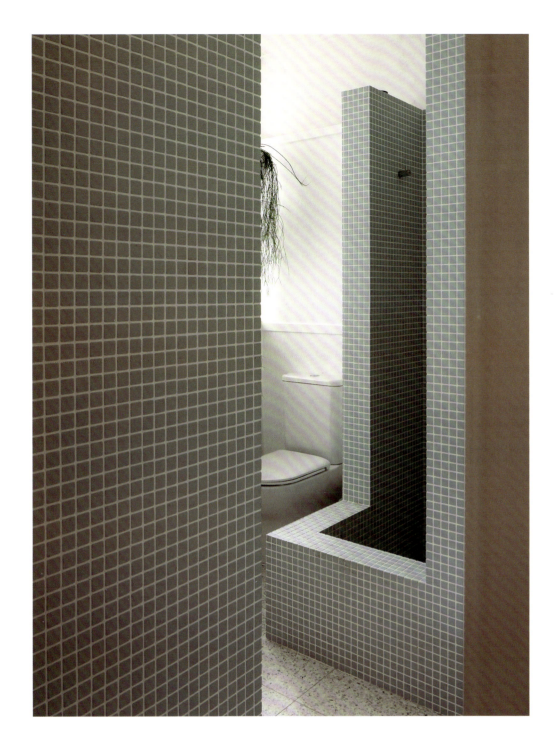

Alexander House

→ Though its dynamic exterior is commanding, internally Alexander House exudes the casual warmth and unforced elegance of a classically Australian beach house.

Loyal Alexander—Trace Architects

Alexander House

Location	Elsternwick, Victoria
	Boonwurrung Country
Original architect	Ernest Fooks
Renovation date	2018
Renovation architect	Preston Lane
Renovation builder	Sargant Construction
Interior design	Preston Lane
Photography	Derek Swalwell

1957

Brick
Residence

Ernest Fooks–Preston Lane

The imperial estate of Rippon Lea in Melbourne's southern suburbs, having witnessed the city expand since its gold rush construction, was feeling the future in 1956. As the Olympic Games drew near, the Australian Broadcasting Commission sliced off a parcel of land from the grounds and built a new-fangled television studio on its doorstep, while across the way the postwar population boom took its own piece, subdividing adjoining property for new housing. These subsequent streets became a Mid-Century Modern wonderland, as many émigré architects and tradespeople with their modern design ideals carried out commissions and constructed new family homes. Ernest Fooks, a Czech-born architect highly regarded in Melbourne's postwar Modernist movement, designed this particular residence here for the present owner's grandfather around 1957.

In 2006, the patriarch of the family died and they faced a final sell-up of the family home. This familiar, transactional event is often thick with emotion as children let go of their connection to place and can signal a wider neighbourhood erasure as one by one these lovely residences are destroyed for valuable land and developer profit margins. In this instance, fate happily intervened when an adult grandchild stepped up to buy the house with his young family.

The new owners initially undertook some cosmetic changes, though after a decade of living in the house and with the family growing up, they decided to carry out a more comprehensive extension. While keeping the typically humble arrangement of three bedrooms, one living room and one bathroom in the home's original footprint, the new works called for a 'parents' bed/bath/study space' with a revamp of the kitchen and better external access. Having purchased the home for its light and succinct design – described by one visitor as 'like a beautiful apartment' – the owners state that the aim was not to create 'a retro museum' but rather a contemporary home that retained its personality and complemented the crafted detail. This balance of old and new was weighted by the owners' cognisance that three generations of family memory, including father and uncles, were baked into every floorboard and brick.

Local firm Preston Lane impressed the owners, who had interviewed several architects, as most personable and perceptive of the task at hand. It would be up to their creativity and an equally skilled builder to deftly reference and extend the Modernist spaces of Fooks' design, without becoming impractical or a cliché.

The cream brick, so elemental to this home's era-specific sensibility, is lovingly celebrated for its material honesty and has been spared the compulsion of lesser hands that would hastily paint it over in dark colours or render it beyond all recognition.

The demolition of a freestanding garage at the back freed up land to construct the new additions, establishing greater privacy in the yard and prioritising the light of the northern orientation. The salvaged brick was repurposed for a new wall separating the new wing from the reorientated kitchen. This divider, an endearing reference to mid-century gapped bond patterns, is further embellished with white metal and glass inlays. Recycled too were original handles, discovered in the garage and utilised once more on internal cabinetry, as well as the glass sliding shelf doors, which were relocated from the original kitchen to the refurbished laundry.

Colour choices are a Doris Day love song, with cabinetry in pale lemon and powder blue. Warm white repeats and connects the old and new via ceilings and lining boards, window frames and the new bagged brick section. This choice of white was a practical approach as well as a design aspect, as the architects had reasoned (when the owners initially preferred black-painted window frames) that white absorbs less heat in summer and is, therefore, less likely to lead to the old window frames cracking over time.

Finished outside with the relaxed Modernist landscape of play lawn, crazy paving and grasses, this wonderfully updated residence now exudes an elegant yet casual air. Granted praise and approval from the older family members on completion, it moves into the future, perfect for yet another generation.

Brick Residence

Ernest Fooks–Preston Lane

↑ A circle motif appears within the new concrete ceiling connecting the original home to the revamped kitchen and running the length of the new build.

← The new addition contains a parents' section with an extra bedroom and bathroom as well as a study, and improves access to the backyard.

Brick Residence

TO LET
108 ACLAND ST.
ST. KILDA
534 0675
talbot
diamond
michelson PTY.

← A sunny pastel reigns supreme in the laundry, with the original kitchen's glass sliding cupboard doors refitted here.

→ Ernest Fooks's legacy is found everywhere in sublimely conceived detail. Security and privacy are translated into a jaunty wrought iron door and dot-reeded glass.

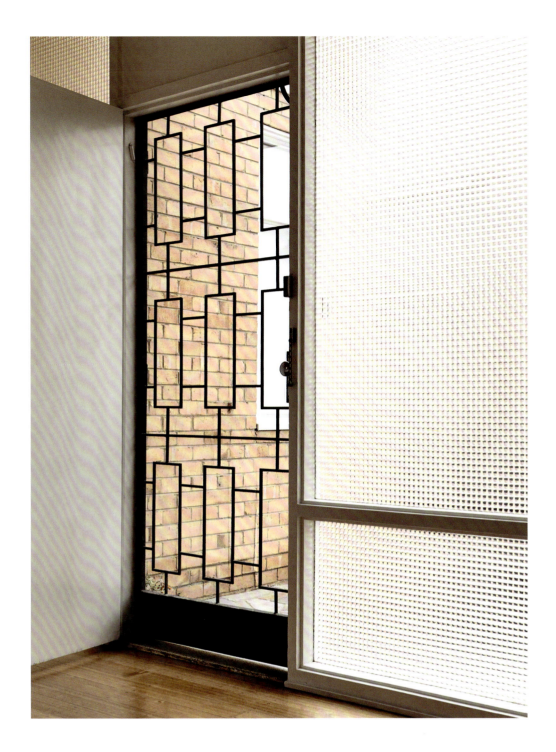

Brick Residence

↑ The old garage was demolished and the bricks reserved to build the dividing wall at the kitchen's end. With a nostalgic bond pattern and white metallic and amber glass inserts, this wall provides a new garage for toy cars.

↘ Modest yet elegant, Brick Residence was described by one visitor before the renovation began as 'like a beautiful apartment'.

→ The joinery in the kitchen is a 1950s Doris Day love song of powder blue and pale lemon.

Ernest Fooks–Preston Lane

← The orientation of the new parents' bedroom makes the most of the natural elements, with the concrete eaves providing shelter in summer but allowing northern sunlight to enter in winter.

→ With its streamlined and accessible design, the new bathroom is a departure from the style of the original home, yet is completed with mosaic tile and classic terrazzo flooring evocative of the Mid-Century Modern era.

Brick Residence

↑   The pared-back Modernist beauty of finely crafted joinery, unadorned brick and large panes of glass is exemplified in the new study nook.

→   A reorientation of the kitchen lengthways opened up the dining and living areas, allowing for casual movement between spaces while ensuring the integrity of Ernest Fooks' original design.

Brick Residence

Location	Grange, South Australia
	Kaurna Country
Original architect	Unknown
Renovation date	2017
Renovation architect	Architects Ink
Renovation builder	Krivic
Interior design	Architects Ink
Landscape design	Architects Ink
Photography	Sam Noonan

1959

GA House

Unknown–Architects Ink

Like many 'garden variety' Australian Mid-Century Modern homes, this architect-designed residence was constructed within an estate, in this instance in Grange, South Australia, in 1959. Catering to a new suburban lifestyle by the beach, it was set back from the road in a T-plan configuration with living–dining quarters up front and a bedroom wing running along the back, all orientated to the central courtyard. Though a relatively simple arrangement, it presented a previously unseen and fresh option to a generation of young families starting out in new peacetime decades. The house survived through the subsequent years during which many of its neighbours became run-down or were demolished, and was acquired by architect Tony Lippis and his interior designer partner, Gina, in the late 1990s with a clear intention of retaining the Mid-Century Modern ambiance while elevating it to a contemporary family home. Family legacy was an additional consideration in this process; the house was purchased from Gina's aunt, whose family had lived there for several generations, adding their own master builder–constructed additions in 1970.

Tony is director of the firm Architects Ink, and his own practice is enmeshed in Modernist principles. The first objectives were to reconfigure the house for an even greater inside–outside flow and to centre the kitchen at its heart. To achieve this, construction began on extra bedrooms at the front, resulting in a new entry. This walkway holds such an unapologetic Mid-Century Modern energy it provokes a sashay on arrival from any visitor. The aforementioned 1970s additions, built in a complementary expression, enclosed the original courtyard to create more interior living space, and their high raked ceilings and exposed timber beams have been embraced with harmonious additional joinery. The kitchen, now at the centre of the house, has large retractable doors that divide the interior from the exterior. New decking encases the backyard pool and its formerly raised concrete border to maximise a single-level outdoor space.

The Lippis' commitment to surfaces that steadfastly wear their spills and scratches – as they call it, 'the patina of life' – ensured the use of unaltered materials, resplendent in inherently natural qualities, in all additions. This includes American oak joinery, fine-grained travertine flooring and stainless steel benchtops. The original slim-line brickwork, an elegant Mid-Century Modern highlight, was a design cue replicated in the newly built sections. The search for this discontinued sixty-year-old brick type spanned the entire country, and only concluded when the sympathetic builder discovered an identical, easily accessible paver to do the job.

The landscaping maintains the philosophy of the renovation, working as an intentionally contemporary garden but with a nod to its mid-century origins. The formation of this garden was subject to its own instances of repurposing and renewal. Waist-height planter boxes running the length of an original front wall, for example, were removed by necessity to increase glazing to full height but reemerged rebuilt along the entry walkway. These were paired with an opposing, stone-filled bed, containing cooling monstera and elephant ear palms. The Lippis' aversion to lawn nature strips and their dependency on less-than-sustainable watering and bothersome mowing called for planting out the entire nature strip with an assortment of easy-care textural favourites. The serendipity of salvage stepped in here with many large agaves requiring removal from the poolside out back relocated to the front. In addition, Tony's discovery of a beautifully mature frangipani tree on a nearby demolition site led to perhaps the most heroic act of the project. With the bulldozer a mere twenty-four hours away, it was duly rescued and transplanted to a primary position in the front garden, converting this stunning botanical marvel from landfill to sculptural centrepiece. This is a nice metaphor for the residence overall, a place that in the wrong hands would also have become rubble and its family history erased but now with love and skill secured. As the owners state, 'The remodelled home suits the family's needs while maintaining the spirit of what has now become a family heirloom.'

GA House

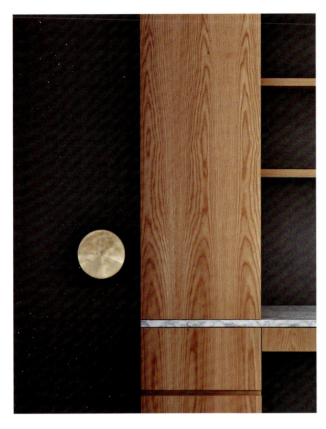

↑ The owners relish the use of natural materials that wear their knocks and scratches with an aged nobility or, as they put it, 'the patina of life'.

→ The new kitchen features sliding glass panels and decking raised to the pool edge to allow seamless indoor–outdoor movement.

Unknown–Architects Ink

GA House

Unknown–Architects Ink

↑   The kitchen was relocated by the owner–architect to the heart of the home, providing consummate place-making for a contemporary lifestyle.

←   The new extension towards the front of the home places bedrooms along an entry path adorned with greenery and slimline brickwork.

→   The casual concealment of tech and promotion of understated utility can be seen in this kitchen, with its minimalist appliance profiles and stove exhaust built into the joinery.

← The interplay of natural light and shade abound in this 'new old' home, hitting a peak in this new bathroom.

→ Old masonry merges with more contemporary materials that echo Mid-Century Modernist flair, including a circular metal door handle, tapware and mosaic tiles.

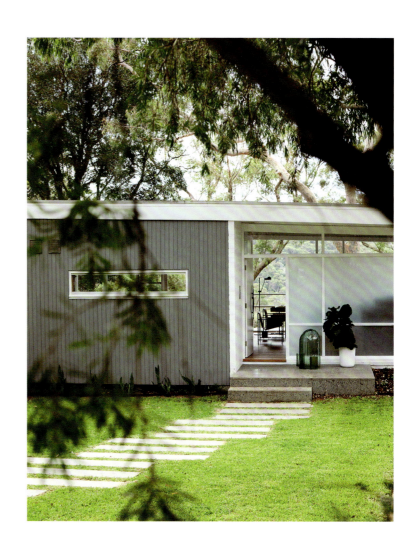

Location	Middle Cove, New South Wales
	Cammeraygal Country
Original architect	Glynn Nicholls
Renovation date	2018
Renovation architect	8 Squared
Renovation builder	Arthouse Projects
Interior design	Studio Gorman
Styling	Claire Delmar
Photography	Prue Ruscoe

1959

The Quarter Deck

Glynn Nicholls–8 Squared

A reminder of each unique narrative present in any renovation project, this example holds fast at a particular end of the high-life scale. In good condition and set in a stunning bushland amphitheatre by the glint of Fig Tree Cove, this home already existed in a rarified realm before this project began. As the family residence of architect Glynn Nicholls, a Mid-Century Modern practitioner with a familial connection to Walter Burley Griffin, the design pleasingly held onto its dynamic form, including a butterfly roofline and many original details, over the decades. Having undergone a succession of renovations and ownership since 1959, it eventually passed into the hands of an American tech exec and his family in 2017.

With a brief to update its inbuilt technological utility (naturally) and double the accommodation for visitors en masse yet hold a sense of cosiness when inhabited solo, the architects and designers so engaged had a task on their hands. Holding clear vision and a certain restraint while carrying out sizeable additions can be a tricky business for any domestic work, with surrender to excess always lurking. The approach here required each discipline to embody a relaxed, gentle reverence which, in the final result, deftly marries the mid-century chic with the prescribed luxury and breadth to outstanding success.

The built extensions of the project, including the carport, sleeping quarters and new main suite, are conceived by the architects in character with the original, forming a seamless transition, as if they have always been there. Suzanne Gorman, principal of the interior design group Studio Gorman, extends upon this with her remit of forming cohesion between old and new, interior and exterior, with considered material choices and select pieces. Adjustments to soften the interiors by replacing scores of downlights with strategic pendant lighting and swapping out glossy floorboards for lightly oiled oak and accompanying joinery embody this temperate attitude.

A singular, warm white permeates inside and out, elevating the refurbished original timber windows and the classic 1950s patterned brickwork at the entry. This section also showcases the original vertical shiplap, repeated in the new study nook.

Though thoroughly elegant, the overarching neutral scheme pops with the joys of the owner and the celebration of its era. The owner's pride, a sunshine yellow VW combi van visible from inside the house, is but the first stop of Mondrian primary yellow, blues and reds, a Mid-Century Modern touchstone, appearing throughout. The playful detailing culminates in a wine room, a dark contemporary retreat, made accessible via a secret, blonde bookshelf.

Externally the landscaping and extended decking happily incorporate the stunning forms of huge gum trees instead of removing them, and allows for seamless, intuitive access to the outdoors and poolside – a remarkable achievement in contemporary Australia's regulatory mire of pool-fencing and bushfire codes.

The attentive respect for the unparalleled natural beauty of the site, with its Mid-Century Modern legacy, is proudly underpinned with a casual sensibility. The final work here is an astounding and ultimately very Australian example of luxury, as beautifully fresh and informal as it is sumptuous.

Glynn Nicholls—8 Squared

↑   Beautiful little pieces fit comfortably into the whole.

←   The architect and interior designer took on the tricky remit of making the home all at once accommodation for many, and a cosy place for a solo inhabitor.

← Shunning the pre-Modernist street-facing convention, all living spaces are positioned to take in the incredible view at the back.

→ A secret door in the bookshelf leads to a hidden bar – but of course.

Glynn Nicholls–8 Squared

Glynn Nicholls–8 Squared

↑ The previous high-gloss flooring and excess downlights have been replaced by new oiled floorboards and strategic pendants.

← Floor-to-ceiling glazing in the open dining area connects residents with the property's arboreal beauty and brilliant sunlight.

→ Art finds its way into every nook of the home, with the neutral palette providing a perfect backdrop.

The Quarter Deck

← Feature tiles and white walls evoke a warm-climate tranquility in more secluded spaces.

↙ Understated luxury underscores the bathrooms.

↓ Playful family accommodation is expressed as bold bunks, tiles and furnishings.

→   Mondrian yellow shines here on joyful, graphic wall tiles.

↘   Deep-blue Flowerpot pendant lights, a design by Verner Panton from 1969, work as ambient or reading lights in the bedroom.

↓   The pop of red, along with the blue and golden yellow, are an intentional reference to the palette of 20th-century titan, Piet Mondrian.

← The Flowerpot lighting convention pops up in this bedroom as a desk lamp.

→ The blue-wash shiplap of the home's facade is repeated here in a study nook, accompanied by simple oak shelving.

Ivanhoe East House

1960

Location	Ivanhoe East, Victoria
	Wurundjeri Woi Wurrung Country
Original architect	Hipwell, Weight & Mason
Renovation date	2020
Renovation architect	Pop Architecture
Renovation builder	Caple Builders
Interior design	Pop Architecture
Photography	Willem-Dirk du Toit

Hipwell, Weight & Mason—Pop Architecture

The middle-ring suburbs of major cities, with their meandering streetscapes and lines of neatly kept homes, hold their histories with an almost unnerving silence. Aside from local children and busybody neighbours, the unintended insularity assures narratives of buildings and lives go unnoticed, fading into the ether over the years. However, in rare instances, some histories are brought back to a new audience, often paired with the astonishment of that which hides in plain sight.

Take this stunning example in the bushy escarpments of Ivanhoe East. In 1959, architectural firm Hipwell, Weight & Mason, a Mid-Century Modern powerhouse, designed this residence in a refreshing Modernist style and then subsequently suffered tragedy as two of the partners prematurely died within eight years of the house's construction, putting an end to that business altogether.

The house was instantly included in a notable list by Mid-Century Modern architect and luminary Neil Clerehan in his formative survey for the Royal Australian Institute of Architects, *Best Australian Houses* (1961). That said and done, this building proceeded to quietly fulfil its intended use as a family residence, seeing through a number of generations and standing as a sentinel of a certain design period, yet widely unnoticed on its hillside.

The present owners, drawn to its spaces, acquired the house as a young family in the mid-1990s and made alterations to suit their immediate needs, extending upon some precursory changes. Thirty years later, with no intention to relocate, the self-same owners entered a new phase, hosting adult children and now grandchildren, and looked to refresh their spaces as a continued family focal point.

As fate would have it, one of these adult children was a builder with local connections to the firm Pop Architecture, leading to their engagement with the project. Foundational research by the architects uncovered the aforementioned Clerehan list with original plans. Along with material cues and the owners' intention to keep the era-specific lines without wading into retro cliché, these plans informed the works, which were primarily concerned with upgrading the kitchen, living room and bathrooms.

Redirecting the focus of the main living space outwards to the impressive vista across the parkland was a central principle. This called for the reversal of additions that had blocked the sightlines, specifically removing the wall between the living room and kitchen. This open space had once been divided with a vinyl concertina screen, long since done away with. The concept was revived with a new sliding partition finely crafted in timber and reeded glass, the architects restoring an enhanced flexibility of the space and greater view via an elegant reimagining of the original architects' design.

Other details of origin are similarly pinpointed and elevated, such as the blue-specked terrazzo tiles in the bathroom, a contemporary match for the 1960 terrazzo shower base in the main ensuite. The reeded glass found in the laundry and bathrooms is now feature glazing in the main living. The blue wall tiles and pink bath of the main bathroom are a nostalgic configuration for anyone of a certain age, rejigged with sympathetic joinery and the pleasing zing of French blue tapware. The new kitchen, taking cues from the original layout, assumes a neutral lightness to balance out the moody depth of the interior timbers and original parquetry.

The owners' longstanding patronage of Australian business and design completes the work to a tee, with Australian Modernist legacy pieces alongside light fittings and tapware from local design businesses, while the walls are adorned in expressive artworks by First Nations practitioners. This creative response to legacy and family duly celebrates both in a self-assured and achingly beautiful outcome and stands as an inspiration for the many secret, and not-so-secret, mid-century suburban houses in our midst.

→ The new kitchen, revised in line with the original, was finished with a neutral lightness to balance out the moody depth of parquetry flooring and internal timbers.

Hipwell, Weight & Mason–Pop Architecture

Ivanhoe East House

← Considered alteration makes for changes that are essential and therefore lasting. In this renewal, no modifications were made apropos of nothing.

→ The owners are great supporters of Australian art and design and have dotted their home with their beautiful collection of works both old and new.

Ivanhoe East House

Hipwell, Weight & Mason-Pop Architecture

↑   Timber takes centre stage, with bespoke wall-fixed cabinets, internal panelling and parquetry projecting timeless elegance at every turn.

←   New works in the main living space redirect the eye out to the impressive parkland vista, enhanced by the removal of previous additions that had blocked sightlines.

← A philosophy of retention is perhaps most obvious in the central bathroom, where the original blue tiles and pink bath have been retained and the bathroom refreshed with the lightest touch.

↙ The pleasing zing of replacement tapware in French blue.

↓ This horizontal formation of above-height windows, sliding mirrored cabinets and benchtop with a perpendicular bath is a Mid-Century Modern layout that pings with nostalgia for people of a certain age.

→ The new terrazzo flooring was matched to the original shower base, a typically demure mottle of grey, blue and white, in the main bedroom's ensuite.

Ivanhoe East House

Torbreck Apartment

1960

Location	Highgate Hill, Queensland
	Turrbal and Jagera Country
Original architect	Job & Froud Architects
Renovation date	2017
Renovation architect	KIN Architects
Cabinetmaker	William McMahon
Interior design	KIN Architects
Photography	Christopher Frederick Jones

Job & Froud Architects–KIN Architects

p. 126   The sophisticated, 'future as now' Torbreck was the first high-rise apartment block ever built in Queensland.

p. 127   Underpinning the finished work is this blue carpet. Laid across most of the apartment, it nods to the blue patinas originally used throughout the complex and those of the cosmos.

←   KIN Architects were drawn into this project via cabinet-maker William McMahon, whose wonderful bespoke handiwork dots the apartment, including this wall joinery.

To our civic detriment, apartment living in this country has never truly secured a foothold as it has in other parts of the world. A thousand cultural excuses and the psychological endlessness of country has seen us paradoxically cling to large cities on the coast yet crave and construct predominantly low-density housing. That said, in the 1950s, when global Modernist ideas were triumphantly ascendant, even Australia looked towards a space-age future of city life in shiny towers. Enter Torbreck, Queensland's first ever high-rise apartment block, which was conceived by developers in 1957 prior to Brisbane council even having planning ordinances for unit living, though keenly aware, even then, of the need to curtail urban sprawl. The project's development, construction and advanced marketing at the time hailed 'the future as now' for owners, most of whom bought off the plan or hoped to (fun fact: in 1958 'Torbreck' was the most popular lottery syndicate name in Brisbane).

A combined vision of unyielding International Style and North American Modern jazzy, the apartment tower design incorporates a material palette of textured brickwork, mosaic walls, steel louvred windows, tiled private balconies and amenities such as built-in appliances and a lush subtropical communal garden and kidney-shaped pool. The architects charged with the development, Job & Froud Architects, were of true Modernist pedigree, ensuring the essentials of orientation, considerable airflow and heat regulation applied to each version of accommodation on offer, from the penthouses to two-bedroom units and bedsits. These apartment options themselves indicate a statement of postwar egalitarianism, promoting a cohabitation of lifestyle varieties in one befitting compound.

While many other Mid-Century Modern block apartments fell out of favour at the end of the last century, Torbreck held onto its glamour, finally earning a heritage listing in 1999, though within it many of the units were tired and/or had been unsympathetically updated. In 2009 a one-bedroom Torbreck apartment was purchased by an owner who, though not quite across the history, was nonetheless attracted to its light and 'vibe'. Following the classic narrative of Mid-Century Modern ownership, this undefined feeling transformed into passion, resulting in an upgrade for the now couple to a three-bedroom apartment a few years later.

In 2017 and through the influence of consummate cabinet-maker William McMahon, the owners consulted with KIN Architects, initially to discuss their thoughts on extending a kitchen island bench. The architects' preliminary sketches and conversations with their clients resulted in further explorations to functionally enhance the whole apartment while honouring its origins, and this led to a larger, more encompassing renovation.

Navigating a tricky set of spaces, the architects focused on cultivating gathering places for dining, talking and relaxing within the whole, drawing the gaze to the high-rise view and adding stunning details to embody the clients' brief of space-age chic.

The physical realities of renovating an older apartment were confronting but not insurmountable. The addition of a minimal yet ingenious timber screen unified disjointed walls and immovable bulkheads and provided extra storage, while a realignment of the kitchen and dining area made the most of the existing timber plinth. Retention of valuable materials, a concern for all involved, saw marble from an earlier renovation seamlessly integrated into the kitchen benchtop and stunning bespoke cabinetry. The space-age charm is dialled up with metallic surfaces bouncing natural light, a pill-shaped wall relief to site all switches and sputnik motifs in the lighting and kitchen exhaust. Underscoring the whole scene is the low-pile blue carpet, the architects' suggestion, tapping into the design legacy of the building with its now faded blue-tiled features, adding a cosmic field of colour and also unifying the past with the updated, more cohesive present.

This apartment now truly embodies the developers' original, optimistic pitch way back in 1957 and inspires today as a statement of Modernist futurism, a pad of allure way up high in the sky.

The architects were originally engaged to configure a new kitchen bench, but the project grew in scope to embrace the entire apartment. Their holistic design work delivers practical necessities that are simultaneously space-age chic.

Torbreck Apartment

Job & Froud Architects–KIN Architects

← The built-in timber shelving units perfectly align with the Mid-Century Modern aesthetic while ensuring adequate storage for a home in which space is at a premium.

→ Torbreck's original architects, Aubrey Job and Robert Froud, were consummate Modernists in their promotion of airflow, natural light and views for each apartment; their elemental design stands up today.

Torbreck Apartment

←   As shown on a poster in the hallway, marketing language for Torbreck presented the units as a 'New Concept in Modern Living', a wondrous proposition for little postwar Brissy and one intensively promoted by its developers.

→   Repurposing materials from earlier alterations was just one aspect of the working philosophy of all parties, giving rise to this marble vanity in the bathroom.

Location	Anglesea, Victoria
	Wadawurrung Country
Original designer	Unknown owner–builder
Renovation date	2021
Renovation architect	Lian
Renovation builder	Michael Russell
Interior design	Lian
Photography	Ben Clement

Early 1960s

Anglesea
Cabin

Unknown–Lian

Coastal hamlets up and down the length of Australia have, in recent decades, witnessed a dramatic change in their natural state and cultural aura. Once, pastel-toned shacks of simple Modernist lines and rambling gardens dotted the landscape, humble abodes existing merely to facilitate holidays around surf breaks, beach cricket and fish 'n' chips. But that is no longer. Any place wildly coastal and a half-day drive from any Australian capital has become quarry to commodification, advancing from all angles via aspirational luxury homeowners and short-stay investors. As the financial value of land rockets skywards, each new height adds crushing destructive pressure on this unique environment and character.

At the crossroads of this change sits this resplendent little cabin. Atop a hill surrounded by nature reserves, it is a generational legacy – held within the same family since the early 1960s. The owner recalls, as a child, his parents planting one particular gum tree that now stands 15 metres tall by the front deck. Constructed without fuss from a basic project plan, this beach house played host to family holidays for decades.

Now retired with adult children of his own, this owner had sought to make this serene spot a more semi-permanent affair, with life changes and the rigours of the recent pandemic allowing for more flexible working locations. The first ideas for a predictable extension doubling the house's footprint were mulled but eventually fell away, replaced instead with a simpler, more elegant concept of restoration and improvement, making for a robust residence, fit for all seasons and stays.

Along with the architect, the builder, residing in the same street no less, maintained impeccable deference to the entire bush and coastal environs and the placement of the home within them, an important facet in the approach and execution of the project. Externally the original cedar cladding was kept, the builder contesting that nothing could withstand the salty coastal bluster better, and also cognisant that any preferred material refitting would not pass the strict bushfire codes of this historically afflicted region.

The classic timber multi-panelled windows were retained, refurbished and repainted white against the dark timber exterior, the thin 1960s panes replaced with double glazing. A complete insulation program was initiated for ceilings, walls and floors, greatly extending the thermal performance of the house as a year-round home, especially in winter months. This upgrade results in not only environmentally astute and economic benefits but also wholly enhances interior comfort for the residents, elevating the immeasurable pleasure of naturally temperate spaces over the merely aesthetic.

Internally the plasterboard came down, replaced with stunning ash cladding, and overhead lighting was eschewed for wall sconces, fostering the architectural concept of residing within the bushland itself and redirecting attention to the view outwards, rather than sequestration in some highly lit capsule.

The removal of the interior surfaces prompted the rescue of one small section, the family height chart, a deeply affecting sliver of memory and tradition, which now sits framed by the dining table. This internal peel-back also revealed the triangular motif of the steel structural beam, now highlighted in white paint as a classic Mid-Century Modern design element.

The salvage continues most nostalgically in the bathroom, with the thoughtful retention and repositioning of the blue bathroom sink. This pastel tone reverberates in the new blue tiles of the bathroom, kitchen and installed wood heater. The reeded glass and plain joinery likewise echo the original, acknowledging the emotional resonance such material detail plays within a place of beloved, generational holiday making.

Anglesea Cabin

← Now well insulated, this home is perfectly liveable in the peak of summer but also during the bracing chill of southern windswept winters.

→ Stripping back the interior revealed the triangular metal truss, typical of this type of construction and era. Painted in white, this practical element has been treated as a design feature in the renewed home.

Unknown–Lian

↑   Recreation outside in the elements lies at the heart of the Mid-Century Modernist beach house, built purely to facilitate holidays of surf breaks, beach cricket and fish 'n' chips.

←   Though this renovation originally included a large extension, the final project has pared the cabin back, seeking to bolster the liveability of the spaces while keeping to the original modest size and form.

↑   A lighting plan of strategically placed wall sconces furthers the concept of residing within the bushland itself, drawing the gaze towards the environment outside.

↘   New tiles in blue are utilised in the bathroom and around the wood heater in the living room in a complimentary nod to the 1960s colourway.

→   The original blue sink has been repurposed in the refurbished bathroom along with reeded glass windows, both holding significant emotional resonance for those who have lived and holidayed here for over fifty years.

Anglesea Cabin

Location	St Kilda, Victoria
	Boonwurrung Country
Original architect	Unknown
Renovation date	2019
Renovation architect	WOWOWA Architecture & Interiors
Renovation builder	Peter Sak
Interior design	WOWOWA Architecture & Interiors
Photography	Martina Gemmola

1960s

Modo Pento

Unknown–WOWOWA Architecture & Interiors

St Kilda, once a Victorian high-stepper gone to seed and nowadays predictably gentrified, is a historical locus of two urban ingredients: multi-dwelling living and midnight revelry. Here, the early 20th century bore witness to a progression of stately, gold-rush mansions lining that one, sweet promenade being converted into boarding houses. Privileged families long fled, their rooms henceforth were taken up, postwar, by the émigré crowd of artists and musicians. The European sophistication of late-night cafes and music sat alongside the thrills of Luna Park and the rising number of Modernist apartment blocks fashioning a street-life vibrancy unseen elsewhere in the city.

So naturally, a St Kilda stalwart was at a party when she quizzed friends for professional recommendations to update her late 1960s penthouse apartment. WOWOWA Architecture & Interiors were name-dropped and took up the project, initially the small task of adding some structure and flexibility to the ill-defined spaces. The apartment itself, situated at the top of a three-storey complex, had been extended upstairs with a bar room and patio on the otherwise under-utilised concrete rooftop. Unusually spacious, the residence overall has multiple bedrooms and two bathrooms, making it already a sizeable family home.

Even so, when mulling a renovation, the finite parameters of any apartment call for intensive planning and rationalisation. Luckily Monique Woodward, principal architect at WOWOWA, relished the challenge as 'the ultimate in spatial problem solving', ensuring that every aspect, from the built-in joinery to wall removal and furniture placement, works overtime to justify its being.

As a solid Mid-Century Modern apartment block, the building possessed inherent qualities for temperature regulation, including double brick walls and the thermal mass of concrete slabs. Modifications in this vein included installing double-glazed windows, a new heating and hot water system, a solar array on the roof and retractable shading. The architect considers this environmental safeguarding as 'a given, a non-negotiable' so intrinsic to any of their work as to not call for lengthy explanations.

As it went along, the brief evolved to encompass supplanting the normcore 1990s renovation with more exuberant interiors relevant to the building's Mid-Century Modern history and character. Emboldened by the client's appetite for adventure, her preference for blue and a mindset for postwar Melbourne optimism, the architect found inspiration popping from sources such as cupcakes, prawn cocktails and the Tupperware of 1960s housewifery. Woodward freely admits to colluding with the enthusiastic builder in an ever-escalating game of decor 'stacks on', until the interiors ran with teal tile grouting, peacock carpeting, brass flourishes and an upholstered bedhead in washed Yale blue.

The addition of elegantly crafted hardwood joinery and parquetry flooring and the retention of the reeded glass doors accompanies the pop with a distinctly warm, Mid-Century Modern sophistication, tempering the jelly desserts with a neat Scotch. Upstairs these same aesthetics unveil new life on the marvellous rooftop, evoking sun-soaked Riviera lounging under a huge striped awning with pebbled deck and breeze block guardrail.

This unapologetically bold renovation is a memorable work of Mid-Century Modern verve captured, contemporised and released in triumph back to its spiritual home, from which the owners and onlookers alike draw immense pleasure. May the party never end.

→ The warmth of crafted timber and the use of metallic and corrugated surfaces lend sophistication to the living space.

Unknown–WOWOWA Architecture & Interiors

Modo Pento

← The daring blue mosaic tile reaches next level with the ingenious (and under-utilised) application of brightly coloured grout to astounding effect, here in the kitchen and elsewhere in the bathrooms.

→ Metallics, elegant timbers and bright mosaics recall the kitchens in the nearby homes of European mid-century arrivals, displaying a unique richness and zest.

↑   Texture, structure and privacy have
    been added to the main bedroom
    on the bottom level.

→   Sliding glass doors remain a familiar
    feature in the homes and spacious
    apartments of this era, enabling
    flexibility and utility. The reeded glass
    adds a certain panache to this relatively
    prosaic solution.

Modo Pento

← The upstairs room, which extends out to a glorious rooftop patio, had been an ill-defined space containing a bar. It has been given new functionality through its refurbishment in keeping with the floor below.

Modo Pento

↑   A gorgeous upholstered bedhead and timber joinery tie in with the apartment's natural surfaces and thematic blues in a stylish, restful retreat.

↘   The architect wryly admits to playing an escalating game of 'stacks on' with the builder, resulting in ever more wild ideas, like this metallic toilet roll station.

→   Wall-mounted sink, utilitarian cabinets and the visual flux of bright mosaic tile each hark back to the era of this apartment's mid-century age.

159   Modo Pento

Beachcomber House

1963

Location	Faulconbridge, New South Wales Dharug and Gundungurra Country
Original architect	Nino Sydney, project plan 'Beachcomber Mk 2'
Renovation date	2014
Renovation architect	Nino Sydney and owners
Renovation builder	Owner–builder
Interior design	Owners
Landscape design	Owners
Photography	Alicia Taylor, courtesy of Modern House Estate Agents

Nino Sydney–Nino Sydney and owners

In 2008 aspiring tree changers Sarah and Billy stopped for respite on a Blue Mountains drive, chancing upon a year-old real estate listing in a discarded newspaper. The keen Mid-Century Modern aficionados zeroed in on the house's audacious profile and knew a call to the agent was in order. A visit to this dilapidated and unsold estate, festooned in danger tape, quickly ensued. Unable to venture inside for safety reasons, the pair nonetheless concluded their trip by paying a deposit, the days of home affordability in a Sydney commuting zone in their final golden hour.

The unmistakeable character of this residence, with its sweeping clifftop view, puzzled Billy, who prodded the architectural fraternity over months to pinpoint its origins. Finally, the name Nino Sydney emerged and this forgotten Modernist architect and his family soon made themselves known to the new owners.

Lend Lease, the 1960s project plan company, was founded like many others of its era to service the postwar housing boom that saw by 1960 a shortfall of close to 400,000 houses in Sydney alone. Employing young innovative architects such as recent Croatian émigré Nino Sydney, the company presented a suite of house plans, most famously at their 1962 Carlingford Homes Fair. (See page 196 for a 'Nino Sydney inspired' plan from this event, Kirriemuir House.) Purchased over the counter by fledgling families seeking their own Australian dream, this plan, the 'Beachcomber Mk 2', was fixed at a build price of no more than two family cars at the time.

The architect conceived this dynamically raised pavilion of brick, timber and glass horizontals for quick and easy construction – a matter of months – and several hundred of the 'Beachcomber', its successor the 'Mk 2' and others resembling it were ultimately built across the country. The new owners fell into an easy consultative relationship with the original architect, and Sydney reassured them they could repair the home themselves with him overseeing the changes, thanks to his intimate knowledge of every piece.

First came the task of replacing many of the termite-riddled Oregon beams. On Sydney's advice, new beams came via salvage from a Northern Beaches carport of the same era, a construction known to have utilised the same timber. With the help of a ladder set on top of a car and some soap to oil the beams, they slid them into the house, their installation restoring the home's integrity and strength. A risky balancing act of tethering the front deck with ropes in order to replace old boards in situ soon followed.

The acrobatics completed, and the perfunctory renovation jobs of rewiring, insulation and other integral works soon realised, the task of the decor came next. As visual artists with a trove of Mid-Century Modern ephemera to their names, there were no half-measures from Billy and Sarah. Bold colours and varied textures of the 1960s are everywhere, exuberant and exulting of their time. Seagrass wallpaper and dotted pegboard feature on walls and shag rugs adorn polished floorboards. The Oregon beams provide a dark linear structure supporting the sky-blue facade and interiors of warm pink and orange. Parker furniture, woven curtains and Murano glass ashtrays further set the scene, while the bathroom remains true to the original, a nostalgic picture of darling mauve tiles and sunny lemon fixtures.

As the changes came together, the original architect in all his European pragmatism and directness watched on as these newfound comrades slowly brought his early work back from a near-total loss to a celebration. In renovation, these owners created a stunningly desirable home for themselves and others but, in addition, their reverence for Modernist design and the era also restored Nino Sydney's name and the concept of project plan houses to their rightful place in the Modernist Australian story. By the time of the architect's death in 2022, this legacy had been secured and an iconic design was now keenly coveted – a valuable and satisfying outcome by any metric.

↑   A riot of bold colour and daring 1960s trends typifies this project overall; here a red fridge sits next to a pink wall oven beside burnt orange walls in the small but inherently practical kitchen.

↘   Iconic Mid-Century Modern pieces appear throughout the house, including an atomic clock, shag rug and saucer pendant light in the living room.

→   The simplicity of the design allows for open-plan living spaces bathed in natural light via floor-to-ceiling windows.

Nino Sydney–Nino Sydney and owners

← This bedroom is a sunny-side vision board for any veritable Jan Brady.

→ The owners revived the bathroom by simply cleaning it up and repairing a couple of cracked tiles to return it to its original lavender and lemon freshness.

Beachcomber House

↑ Textiles complete the picture, with window furnishings displaying a dynamic array of retro geometric patterns and loose, open weaves of textural experimentation.

→ The replacement ceiling beams were slid individually into the building with the help of a car, a ladder and some soap, re-establishing the structural integrity of the house.

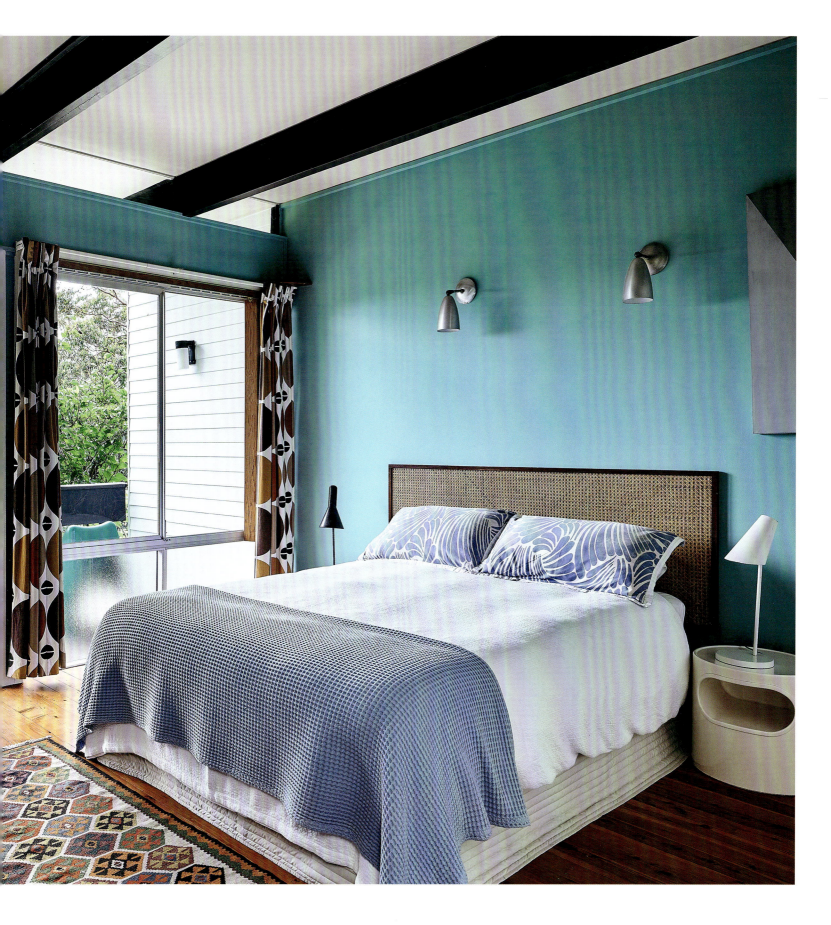

169   Beachcomber House

Location	Frankston, Victoria
	Boonwurrung Country
Original architect	Clarke Hopkins Clarke
Renovation date	2019
Renovation architect	MRTN Architects
Renovation builder	Technique Construction Group
Interior design	MRTN Architects
Photography	Derek Swalwell

1963

Frankston House

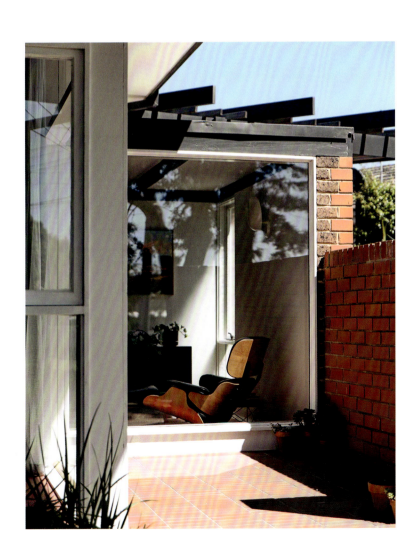

Clarke Hopkins Clarke–MRTN Architects

In outer Melbourne we find a classic example of domestic architecture that embodied the Modernist postwar housing output for the emerging Australian 'suburban family' lifestyle. It was designed and constructed in the early 1960s by new architecture firm Clarke Hopkins Clarke for an engineer colleague and his family, one of the thousands of domiciles desperately required for a new population boom. It bears noting here that this firm's founding partner Jack Clarke was a contributor of home plans to *The Age* Small Homes Service led by the indomitable Robin Boyd, and a year prior to this home's construction Clarke had captained Australian Rules football team Essendon to their 1962 grand final win. Not a bad year's work.

Over the years the house weathered and witnessed fifty-five years of accelerating societal change. And though this local variety of Modernist architecture effectively delivered to Australia the middle-class conventions of open-plan living and indoor–outdoor entertaining, pioneer examples like this one remain at high risk of being destroyed. Relatively small building footprints on large blocks of land, once a haven of gardening, hobbies and children's play, are now a powerful enticement for demolition.

Thankfully this residence was snapped up by owners with a devoted appreciation for Mid-Century Modern architecture and design. They subsequently engaged Antony Martin, principal of MRTN Architects, with the direct intention to renovate the home yet maintain its integrity and the era-specific atmosphere that had attracted them in the first instance.

Though the basic Modernist floor plan of this home, with living and dining spaces separated from the sleeping zones, was part of the appeal, practically speaking the client's brief outlined the need for extra bedroom space and a kitchen that accommodates contemporary cooking and dining as a more social affair. As such, the house was effectively gutted to remove the unsympathetic additions of later decades and allow for an expansion of its form. The ceiling was raised and the exposed beams retained, and the kitchen was remodelled, its orientation flipped lengthways. Expanded access to a northern courtyard was built and bedroom walls were extended outwards.

This deconstructed midpoint and amended floor plan next drew upon careful material choices to reassert the essential nature of this 1960s suburban dream with a nod to West Coast US Modernism. This included surface and decor choices of mosaic tiles in the bathrooms, swirly maple joinery and cedar accents. The floor of the original formal living room is an undeniable 1950s salute in its new pink carpeting. Most stunning of all is the large expanse of Japanese clay-fired floor tiles that span entry to the kitchen through to the living area, a wink to Frank Lloyd Wright and his Asian influences but more pointedly tracing the flow of uninterrupted movement through the home. This intuitive design, an expressly Modernist concept pursued by its original architect, is amplified in elegance and practicality by the new one.

Ideals of salvage and conservation appear most wonderfully here in the original red bricks, which had been discontinued years ago. The builder, knowledgeable about and respectful of this material reality, set to arduously saving, cleaning and resetting spare bricks into walls of traditional jaunty pattern work – yet another delightful mid-century touch worked into the new, which concurrently doubles as bathroom screening.

The clear aspiration in this project, to sympathetically 'reimagine' a residence rather than knock it down and rebuild, is a deliberate decision to walk a more challenging path. The research, patience and skill required for a job well executed is immense but, as we see here, is ultimately more rewarding. Having once saved this home from destruction, the owners have, with the aid of similarly enthusiastic architects and craftspeople, ushered it with joy into a certain future.

Frankston House

← The dining area is bathed in light flowing through windows opening onto a new north-facing courtyard.

→ The kitchen was reorientated to ensure maximum utility and social connection, without increasing the actual floor space.

Clarke Hopkins Clarke–MRTN Architects

↑   The bold, deep pink carpet is a nod
    to the Mid-Century Modern embrace
    of colour in domestic settings.

←   The footprint of the lounge room remains
    unchanged, merely opened up slightly
    to form better spatial connection.

→   A fondness for Mid-Century Modern
    style is evident in the collectables and
    furnishings throughout.

← The new bathroom is shielded by a privacy screen fashioned from bricks steadfastly retained, cleaned and reused by the builder.

→ A palette of timber, whites and dashes of colour balances the contemporary with classic Mid-Century Modern style.

Clarke Hopkins Clarke–MRTN Architects

← A refurbished central bathroom, in its day a revelation of modernity when compared to the old washroom out the back.

↙ A collection of textures in vegetable (indigenous kidney weed) and mineral (Japanese tile and concrete) form.

↓ The bathroom pairing of geometric tile with terrazzo flooring is another example of its happy resurgence in recent years.

→ To address present needs, bedroom walls were pushed out to provide more space and storage.

Frankston House

Location	City Beach, Western Australia Whadjuk Nyoongar Country
Original designer	Unknown owner–builder
Renovation date	2020
Renovation architect	Simon Pendal Architect
Renovation builder	Rossbrook Construction
Structural engineer	Forth Consulting
Interior design	Ohlo Studio
Landscape design	CAPA Studio
Photography	Robert Frith (exteriors) and Jack Lovel (interiors)

1964

City Beach House

Unknown–Simon Pendal Architect

It's a wide open road in any direction to reach or leave Perth, but the geographical realities of one of the world's most remote cities failed to quell the march of Modernist architecture in the 20th century. This is often exemplified by the flamboyant abodes of Bulgarian émigré architect Iwan Iwanoff that stand now as adored landmarks, as synonymous with the city as the surf beaches and overexposed sunlight.

Perth's metropolitan expansion began in the debutant twirl of the 1962 Commonwealth Games, all eyes west propelling the growth of a string of new suburbs, carved out of the bushland. And aside from higher profile architects making their names, tradespeople built the tracts of houses, often bespoke and embodying Modernist design principles to lesser or greater degrees. Regrettably, in civic transformation ushered in via mining wealth and the appeal of the coastal vicinity, scores of these dear little homes have disappeared in recent decades, their humble bearing no match for the desired mega-mansion.

City Beach, a typical suburb of that mid-century growth, is the location of this jaunty residence, built by a figure now lost to history though likely conceived without formal architectural input. Purchasing this home in 2017 for its Modernist bones, the owners sought to create a fresh family home, suitably chic yet deferring to the existing character. A working connection between the owners and Jen Lowe from the interior design group Ohlo led to both Jen and architect Simon Pendal taking the reins of this all-encompassing renovation.

Deconstructed to the point of stripping off every window and door, the asbestos roof and the interior cabinetry and free from any preciousness of noted historical pedigree, the house was ready for the architects and designers to set out a new plan.

Consciously attuned to environmental impact, the spiritual importance of garden and eschewing meaningless bloat, the new internal layout keeps to the exact footprint of the old yet invigorates the spaces with a bright elegance and contemporary usefulness. From the front path, visitation is channelled into a seamless flow through the home's main living zone and then out again, finishing in a curtained rotunda for outdoor entertaining. The feature was part of the brief for the owners, who prioritise social commune wholly ensconced in the magnificent Perth climate.

Landscape design was undertaken by CAPA Studio, who took a boundary-to-boundary approach in an intentionally indigenous palette of textural local grasses, groundcovers, ferns and coolabah trees, expressing altogether a cultivated sand-belt elegance. Dazzling white permeates the palette, along with the yellow of the pathways, not in thoughtless application but as a specific tonal accommodation for the powerful sunlight which dominates this part of the country. Sunbaked, salted and bleached. The architect was similarly inspired by Modernist artist David Hockney's iconic LA series.

Visual cues of Mid-Century Modernism and detail also appear in crafted echoes in the beautifully grained kitchen joinery, alongside the common simplicity of the Parker armchairs in the lounge. Minimal shelving for vinyl records, a timber wall divider and the painted metal balustrades are each a retelling of familiar 1960s features. The garage doors with pop-circle perforations join the dots to the internal window shutters, an ingenious device to allow security and airflow and shadow movement internally.

Though flawless in its presentation, the project – like all renovations of legacy builds – was not without the typical issues of engineering and, along with that, more subtle cultural allowances. The garage, for example, required excavation to allow space for any contemporary car, with SUVs having wholly subsumed the little sedan as Australia's family wagon.

And nearing completion, the ever-unforeseen also sought to raise its head with the advent of the pandemic. Though not greatly impacting on the project, then in its final stages (unlike some others in this book), the rolling closures and all-encompassing uncertainty supercharged the impetus to finish. Understandably for such a residence so close to assuming its total and incredible rebirth, it was only natural that any owners would desire to move in and soak up those stunning spaces as soon as humanly practicable – which in the end, they happily did.

Unknown–Simon Pendal Architect

↑   Recurrence of materials throughout the home is detailed here in the bespoke shelving with a mosaic tiled edge and tube metal legs.

←   Inbuilt seating, a signifier of many a Mid-Century Modernist building, is here given an almost Mediterranean edge thanks to the heft of its concrete form.

← Beautiful crosscut timber is generously utilised in the kitchen cabinetry.

→ Echoes of the nearby desert landscape permeate the art, surfaces and bleached palette of the home.

Unknown–Simon Pendal Architect

← Simple Parker chairs are combined with
contemporary pieces and a cherished
record collection in the lounge.

↓ Another 20th-century speciality –
the bar trolley – appears in a suitably
industrial yet chic variation.

↘ Sculptural characters are dotted
strategically throughout the home.

→ Cooling, clean surfaces of tile temper
the enduring summer heat.

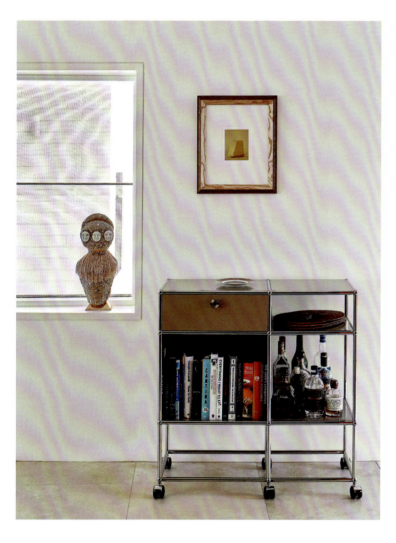

City Beach House

Unknown–Simon Pendal Architect

← The finely crafted two-tone joinery marks
   a division between living spaces.

→ The masterfully built joinery in the main
   bedroom continues the flowing lines of
   the concrete in the living area and deep
   timber grain in the kitchen.

Unknown–Simon Pendal Architect

↑ Landscaping features an indigenous palette of textural local grasses, groundcovers, ferns and coolabah trees.

← The rotunda was an important element for the owners, who prioritise social commune wholly ensconced in the magnificent Perth climate.

→ A sink and barbecue in the new rotunda add extra utility to this outdoor setting.

City Beach House

Kirriemuir House
1964

Location	Hamlyn Heights, Victoria
	Wadawurrung Country
Original designer	Owners, based on Nino Sydney
	project plan 'Pan Pacific'
Renovation date	2017
Renovation architect	Studio 101 Architects
Renovation builder	Chris Mahony, Meridean Builders
Interior design	Studio 101 Architects
Landscape design	Studio 101 Architects
Photography	BWRM Geelong

Owners, based on Nino Sydney project plan–Studio 101 Architects

p. 196   Purchased at an affordable price due to its regional location, this 'Nino Sydney inspired' home, already a neighbourhood celebrity, has been treated to a long overdue revival.

p. 197   Project house plans, though not site specific, promoted Modernist design ideals. Here the indoor–outdoor connection typical of the Australian lifestyle is present in this lovely courtyard.

←   Mid-Century Modernist design, in all its joyful experiments, has been elevated across the home, as seen in the wall of original breeze blocks peeping in from the courtyard.

In 1962 a family from Geelong, Victoria, travelled 950 kilometres to Carlingford, Sydney, to look over the Carlingford Homes Fair, a joint event presented by Lend Lease and *The Australian Women's Weekly* magazine. At the fair, they would have strolled down leafy new streets to gaze at twenty-four examples of the new modern option for a booming, postwar Australia: architect-designed spec homes from the likes of Ken Woolley, Don Gazzard, Harry Seidler and Neville Gruzman. But it was the chief architect of Lend Lease at that time, Nino Sydney, and his five example homes that caught their eye. Upon return, this family, like many others, picked a local builder and constructed their own family home based on Sydney's jaunty 'Pan Pacific' house plan. With this initiative, among others, the dream of fresh modern spaces and luxuries were now affordable for middle-class and blue-collar Australia.

A humble but intuitive design, this three-bedroom variation (in the footprint of the four-bedroom plan, adjusted to make bigger but fewer bedrooms) included architectural elements all at once charming and refreshingly new, including raked ceilings, split levels, an open plan kitchen and large walls of glazing. Also part of the design were relief brickwork, breeze blocks and a feature stone fireplace.

Time-jump five decades and architect Peter Woolard, whose formative years were spent in the offices of the notable firm McGlashan Everist, was looking for a residence amenable to local schooling for his young family. Additionally, this dream home would present as an aesthetically compatible refuge for his and his partner's formidable Mid-Century Modern furniture collection. Stars aligned and they purchased this tired old rental, lovingly referred to as 'The Brady Bunch house' by neighbours, for a regional suburban price tag.

The first two years were spent living in and absorbing the sensibility of this house as a family. Following this, prior to any of the fun stuff, they undertook fundamental work to stabilise the building for future liveability. It was, as Peter says, 'the hard work of fixing all the things you don't see', which included but was not limited to installing a new roof, plumbing, insulation and a heating and hot water service, as well as replacing sections of eaves very carefully lest the asbestos be disturbed. This initial work was often simply a matter of stripping back the layers and exposing the original Modernist allure as intended, such as the relief brickwork at the entry which, when freed from under a thick coat of dull house paint, sang like 1964 all over again.

The second stage of this transformation was the contemplation of life and movement within. What exactly do growing children and two adults require in their personal spaces? Is there truly a need for a second bathroom or ensuite? How best to tweak for maximum functionality or to connect the interiors with the large backyard? How, above all, to achieve this while keeping to a tight budget? Some strategic changes included opening up the bathroom/laundry to create dual access in lieu of another bathroom, and moving a pivotal cupboard in the living room to make space for seating. The former 'formal' dining area was converted to a home office (just in time for a raging pandemic) and each bedroom window was affixed with a sliding door connected to backyard decking. These individual resolutions in completion were achieved without excessive building or any real extension. This reaffirms the staunch discipline from the owners to keep the humble 1964 footprint and to a modest budget.

The final result is an inspirational and particularly joyful embrace of a hip Mid-Century Modern design in all its swingin' spirit, while successfully serving a contemporary family and their needs.

→ Stripping back layers of thick, dull paint has seen this wonderful brick feature wall sing once more like it's 1964.

Owners, based on Nino Sydney project plan–Studio 101 Architects

Kirriemuir House

↑   A light touch refurb was carried out in the kitchen, with much of the original joinery retained and new technology seamlessly integrated.

←   This humble renewal has maintained the typical three-bedroom, one-bathroom format of the house along with its 'ultra Modern' concept of an open living and kitchen area.

↑ The central bathroom was reorientated with extra access points for the family creating greater utility, avoiding the need to build a second bathroom.

→ Bespoke joinery exceeds many a budget and storage can be resolved with off-the-shelf options. Ikea wardrobes were built into the main bedroom, behind the bedhead.

Owners, based on Nino Sydney project plan–Studio 101 Architects

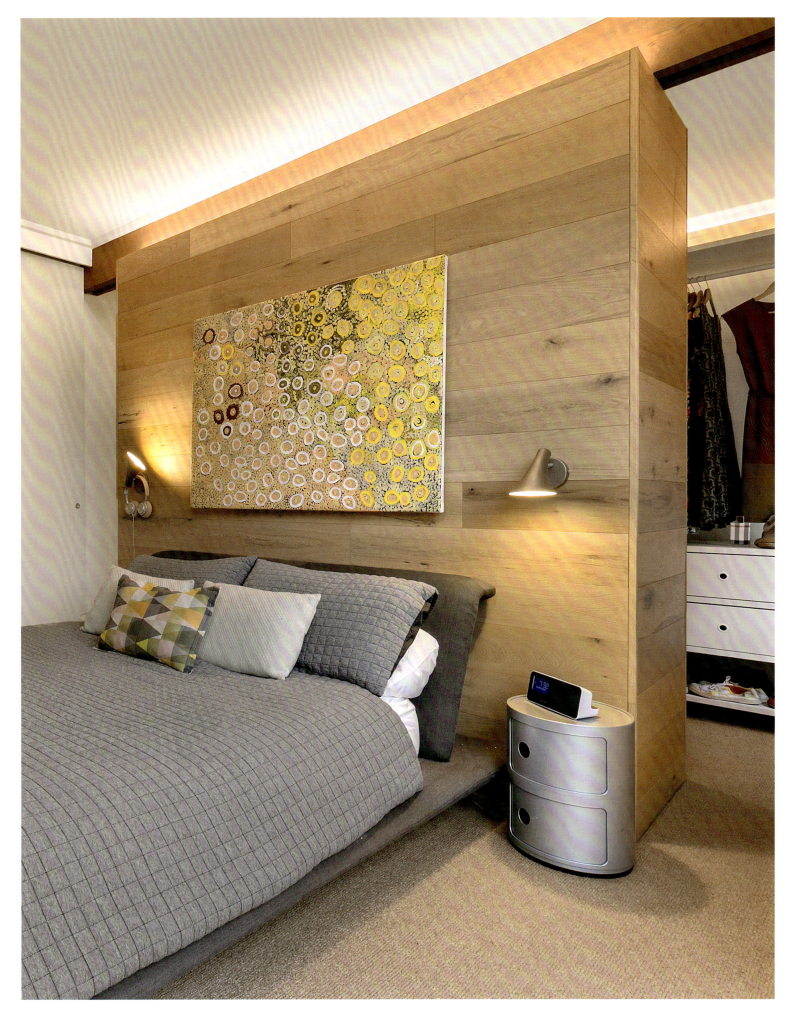

Kirriemuir House

Location	Kenmore, Queensland
	Turrbal and Jagera Country
Original architect	Unknown
Renovation date	2021
Renovation architect	KIN Architects
Renovation builder	A.H. Done Builders
Interior design	KIN Architects
Landscape design	Arbour Essence
Photography	Christopher Frederick Jones

Late 1960s

Kenmore Renovation

208   Unknown–KIN Architects

As inner Brisbane riverside locales, Kenmore and Chapel Hill embodied the promise of the new suburban era in postwar Australia when, in the 1960s, dairy farmland bought by the Hooker group was swiftly developed and the first schools, shopping strips and housing tracts sprang up. These days the area still reverberates with a Generation X childscape of rambling footpaths lined with mature trees, and classic mid-century family homes are still apparent on larger blocks. This particular three-bedroom house, purchased by a professional couple, was certainly liveable from the outset, yet retained under-utilised aspects of its archetypal design. The raised rectangular form holding a commanding horizontal street facade was, in essence, a single-level residence on plinths, hosting all living, bathing and sleeping upstairs. Underneath at ground level was a storey of dirt-floored emptiness next to a carport and a pool disconnected from any interior engagement, and overall a lack of indoor–outdoor spaces.

Having already refurbished the upstairs, the owners desired a thorough rework to make their forever home more responsive to their lifestyle without needless extension of the footprint or diminishing its locale-specific, family vibe. Engaging local firm KIN Architects, the owners gave them a brief to accommodate Lego-building afternoons, extra storage, a biking habit and more cohesive socialising by the pool.

Though recently navigating the renovation of another Mid-Century Modern residence, the Torbreck Apartment (see page 126), the architects took on this new project free of any design baggage, for while this residence is chronologically only a decade younger than Torbreck and in the same Modernist class, it is divergent in aspects of aesthetics, size, purpose and location. This requires of any architect worth their trade a ground-up approach and a completely separate vision.

First came foundation work, including major drainage rectification at ground level and a considered reimagining of connections to the existing amenity in the plans. The joy of selecting a palette and surface materials followed, which, borne from a client's trust in their architects, became ever bolder as the project progressed. Monochrome beginnings evolved into bright orange shelving and eaves, a blue louvred courtyard, splashes of various terrazzo and rich metallic accents.

Central to the project is the ground-floor sunken loungeroom, a compositional device criminally ignored in the past few decades of domestic architecture. This new living space establishes a level interconnection with the pool and embraces the shade in deep, mossy patinas, a cooling response to the subtropical climate. The room is anchored by a bespoke bar, contains storage for any number of collectibles and is sequestered by a hidden panel door off the carport – it is the cheeky crossover of a speakeasy with a 1970s rumpus room.

The position of the kidney-shaped pool remains unaltered in the bright northern yard, its regulation fencing understated and almost invisible in the overall design, a hard-won victory for any new building.

A request for garaging, exercise space and an accompanying bathroom manifests in new utility rooms also at ground level, enabling true ease of transition and storage. The shower room is a nostalgic yet unselfconscious replication of the public pool aesthetic, with simple white tile, louvred window and utilitarian terrazzo. Here, the echo and splash of bombs off the diving board resonate.

The newly enhanced courtyard, directly above the new lounge, continues the connection via the poolside stairway, and is another value-add to a previously underused space, fostering a breezy indoor–outdoor flow for dining and entertaining with the expressly Queensland tradition of louvres and breeze blocks nailing both privacy and shelter from the elements.

Looking from the street, this residence is commanding and whole; however, it is internally and underneath where the cohesiveness of space and daring finishes have been maximised, which brings genuine awe to this renovation. Sympathetically embellished and singularly audacious, this is now a true family and 'forever' home and will be for many years to come.

Kenmore Renovation

← The upstairs area, already renovated in mostly black and white, let loose with the fostering of bold accents, as seen in this orange plastic pendant light.

→ The shower room is a nostalgic yet unselfconscious replication of the public pool aesthetic.

Kenmore Renovation

Unknown–KIN Architects

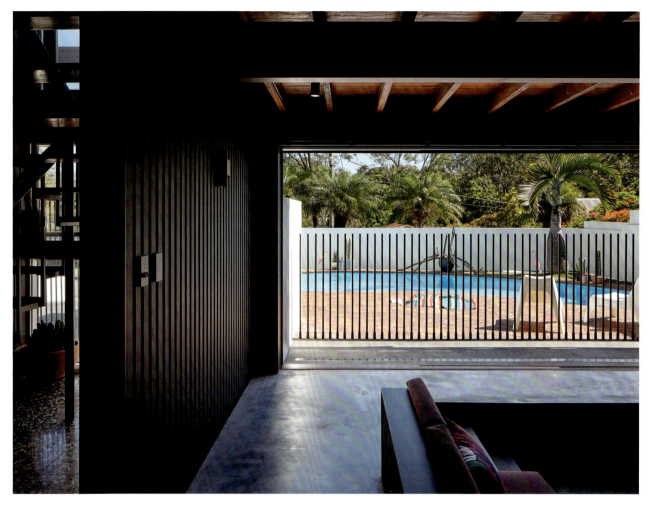

↑   The architectural challenge of establishing the house's connection to the pool while adhering to fencing regulations has been masterfully addressed.

←   In response to the subtropical Queensland climate, the new living area offers respite from the sun with shade-filled zones and darker surfaces.

→   The original kidney-shaped pool is retained in the northern courtyard, this outdoor space made anew due to greater accessibility from the house.

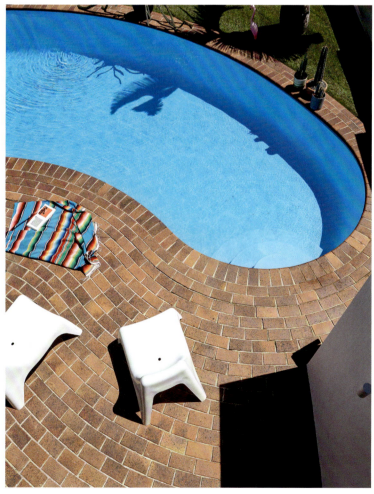

↑ The view from the upstairs courtyard, a space stylishly rejigged by the architects to allow easier access for dining and relaxing with privacy.

→ Louvres, typical of the local Queenslander home architecture for managing airflow and temperature, are partnered with Mid-Century Modernist breeze blocks in this wonderfully revived space.

Unknown–KIN Architects

Location	Warrandyte, Victoria
	Wurundjeri Woi Wurrung Country
Original designer	Alistair Knox
Renovation date	2020
Renovation architect	Adriana Hanna
Renovation builder	Plan Build Co
Interior design	Adriana Hanna
Landscape design	Miniscape Projects
Photography	Sean Fennessy

1969

Fisher House

Alistair Knox–Adriana Hanna

As a companion landscape to the crags and eucalypts of Sydney's bush escarpments, Melbourne's eastern flank of Eltham, Heidelberg and Warrandyte also shares an architectural essence. From the beginning of last century, these farm acres became the playground for all forms of experimental living. Montsalvat and Heide, both established in the 1930s, propagated mid-century Australian bohemia with synonymous names like Sunday Reed, Albert Tucker and Mirka Mora. Moving into the 1960s and 1970s, a younger generation took up bush blocks by the upper Yarra, this cohort similarly seeking to make art, build community and commune with nature. In recent years, the design audience's re-embrace of a crunchier, later Modernist aesthetic in all its browns and bricks has put the spotlight on naval man, builder turned design innovator Alistair Knox. Though technically not a trained architect, Knox's organic vision saw him design over a thousand residences and build hundreds over his career.

When this particularly elegant and well-maintained Alistair Knox house came up for sale, photographer Sean Fennessy and his art director partner Jess Lillico leapt at it, having been looking for just the right 'bush' retreat for eighteen long months. Mindful of the home's legacy, Sean searched the council records for evidence of its provenance, there discovering Knox's plans. Constructed in 1969 as a single-bed home for one, a mysterious Ms Fisher, it was expanded a few years later by the second owners, who sympathetically increased the square footprint with extra bedrooms on one side and a studio and garaging on the other.

Fifty years forward and the third owners too mulled changes to contemporise and repair the residence. As Jess explains, they decided to employ an architect to take on 'the million tiny decisions' required in such a project, which can drain even the most design astute. They ultimately connected with architect Adriana Hanna. Hanna shared an understanding of the house and the desire to delicately adjust it while keeping to its historical, architectural and environmental integrity.

Once the renovation and landscaping plans were confirmed, work was set to start in early 2020, a fateful time indeed. Confronted with Melbourne's covid-related suppression of movement, material shortages and labour delays, the owners rolled with the punches and diverted their energy and weekends into the garden. Removing the overgrowth of introduced greenery, they sought to embrace the texture and grey-green hues of Warrandyte's indigenous flora. Landscape designers Miniscapes stepped up to provide a cohesive vision, resulting in a breathtaking terrain of sandy paths edged in fanning groundcovers, grasses and sculptural blue eucalypts. New terracing and a small children's play lawn better define spaces for social engagement outdoors.

The internal renovation and refurbishment was an exercise in aesthetic kinship. Though the bathrooms and kitchen required repair from natural deterioration and a slight reconfiguration, the material palette and neutrality were upheld. New joinery, including the kitchen bench, comprised compatible timbers and tiles of warm white as per the original.

Creating visual relief from all-encompassing brick and timber are selectively bagged and painted internal walls, a considerably risky act when dealing with original Mid-Century Modern homes. This was, however, approached with reassurance from the architect that it would be of light touch and an organic character recalling Knox's famed mudbrick aesthetic, which it does to perfection, looking for all intents and purposes as original.

The lovely ingenuity of many little details seen in this project is epitomised by the new freestanding divider shelves. This small but important addition expands its utility at every turn, providing much-needed storage and a structure to support bespoke seating for the living room, as well as architecturally enhancing privacy for the main bedroom while presenting a more pronounced entrance at the front door.

By the end of the project, after all the hard work was done, what was once supposed to be a weekender had been so beautifully updated it seduced the owners into a permanent move out of town. This family joins the long tradition of creatives housed in Australia's most organic expression of Modernism, built in harmony with the light, the trees and the air.

Fisher House

← New joinery that was required in wet areas such as the kitchen has been carried out in compatible timbers, and tiled in a neutral warm white, in keeping with the original treatment.

→ Natural light and the outdoors seep in at all angles in the kitchen via internal and external windows, as well as skylights.

Alistair Knox–Adriana Hanna

Alistair Knox–Adriana Hanna

↑ Timber and natural textiles create a sense of warmth and calm throughout the home.

← Bagging the brick walls in certain sections was a risky move but it has been carried out with the utmost precision and deference to the mudbrick character of Alistair Knox's original design.

Alistair Knox–Adriana Hanna

↑   A new divider shelf acts as storage, structure for new seating and privacy screen for the entry to the main bedroom.

←   The seamless integration of seating, shelving and entertainment. No changes were made on the fly; all was considered for purpose, space and ambiance.

→   Tidy nooks allow everything to be in its right place.

← Seagrass wallpaper is another woefully forgotten Mid-Century Modern surface finding welcome use here.

↙ Contemporary fittings and new tapware and sconces create a harmonious whole in the refurbished bathroom.

↓ The tranquility of a bedroom at the golden hour.

Alistair Knox–Adriana Hanna

→ The main bedroom offers immediate access to the garden via a sliding door, an easy evocation of sleeping outdoors, if so desired.

↘ The ageless, eternal quality of textured masonry.

↓ The bathroom, as with the kitchen, has kept its original, natural palette.

Fisher House

Lindfield
House
1969

Location	Lindfield, New South Wales
	Cammeraygal Country
Original architect	Bill Baker
Renovation date	2018
Renovation builder	Varcon Constructions
Interior design	Frank Designs
Photography	Jacqui Turk

Bill Baker–Frank Designs

Plotting escape from a city cottage that grew smaller every day, interior designer Amelia Hasketh, founder of Frank Designs, was searching with her partner for a family home to raise two small children with another on the way. A long stint of inspections eddied around a particular school zone but led nowhere until they walked into this residence designed in 1969 by architect Bill Baker, whose career traversed the glory days of Mid-Century Modern Sydney. He undertook many commissions from the late 1950s with firm Levido & Baker and then solo into the late 1960s, though he also consistently lent his hand to project home designs – he was a recognised practitioner of the form, one might say.

Stepping into the run-down, single-owner home, Amelia and family had to contain their excitement. Though all other prospective buyers expressed the desire to knock it down and rebuild, they were enraptured by the light-filled orientation, cedar panelling and finely crafted joinery, and their resolve to secure the house and revive it was steadfast within the hour.

Upon settling in, the family knew not to move too rapidly with any grand plans until they truly understood the home and its moods. Amelia explains they needed at least one year to 'get all the seasons', in order to track the sunlight, the direction of the breeze, and how the family moved within and used the home. From this intel, they would gain the spiritual blueprint to proceed in practical terms.

After seeking architectural help, with the twin requirements of a strict budget and the retention of the Mid-Century Modern feel, the owners were left unfulfilled. Amelia, having grown up with a father who cherished architecture, and indeed designed his own family home in New Zealand, decided to utilise her own knowledge and skillset for the project.

Strategic demolition set the scene: they removed one wall to open the living and dining area and allow reorientation of the kitchen. The deep timber accents, an integral part of the home's attraction, were embraced with touch-ups in mission brown (yes, the one and only!) paint. Elsewhere they restored the damaged cedar panelling and salvaged every last stick of original timber joinery to either repurpose or refurbish and return in situ, a particularly satisfying outcome for the owners.

Replacing the roof was tricky – because of its zero-degree elevation, an eternal Mid-Century Modern bugbear, tradesmen initially refused any warranty if they rebuilt like-for-like. This was eventually resolved with some tweaking of the roof pitch and has since proven itself, standing leak-free in the greatest rain test of all: La Niña's years-long visitation.

Retrofitting heat, another conundrum in Modernist homes due to minimal ceiling and underfloor cavities, first called for the removal of the fifty-year-old oil heater (complete with a tank full of the stuff) from the back deck and installation of a new electric system carefully integrated, dressed and discreet, in cedar cladding. The central freestanding wood heater came next to add a focal point for the living space, in a contemporary throwback to a Mid-Century Modern convention.

Features in fearless colour, the language of the home's late 1960s age when bold was beautiful, now sees each space projecting its own personality with jade kit kat and deep cobalt tiles, patterned wallpapers or bright green carpet. Rounding out the project is furniture of sympathetic age and robust designs, not so much Modernist museum pieces but rather the middle-Australian comfort of Parker and Fleur, virtually child-proof.

All in all, this project coalesces into a superb family home of a truly embraced Mid-Century Modern past and a warm, inviting future. And though the owners are at present on the other side of the world, they cannot wait to walk in the door and sit in those sunlit rooms, once again.

Lindfield House

→ Mission brown paint, once a punchline in jokes deriding Mid-Century Modern homes, was used on the structural beams to beautifully revive them. Haters begone.

Bill Baker–Frank Designs

233   Lindfield House

↑ The small but serviceable kitchen has been reorientated through the removal of a wall to open it up to the dining space, a strategic change seen in a number of these projects.

→ While retaining the typical timbers and horizontal lines of a 1960s kitchen, this one also includes delightful Japanese kit kat tiles.

Bill Baker–Frank Designs

↑ Retrofitting heating can be tricky. Here split system technology has been enveloped in timber cladding, concealing and updating the addition in a brilliant resolution.

↘ There's always room for a 1960s sideboard topped with a turntable and selection of liquors.

→ Serviceable, child-friendly furniture abounds, bathed in the light of floor-to-ceiling windows.

Lindfield House

Bill Baker-Frank Designs

↑ The use of bold colour continues
in this bathroom with its deep cobalt
mosaic tiles.

← Bold green carpet accompanies the
dark wood in the inviting main bedroom.

← The bathroom features a light, fresh colour palette and ample sunlight.

→ Contemporary wallpaper that speaks to the playful patterns of Mid-Century Modern textiles finds a place in a children's bedroom.

241   Lindfield House

Location	Mount Martha, Victoria
	Boonwurrung Country
Original architect	Karl Fender
Renovation date	2018
Renovation builder	Whelan Project Builders
Interior design	Owners
Landscape design	Owners
Photography	Derek Swalwell

1973

Fender
House

Karl Fender—Owners

As Mid-Century Modern architects and their clients, mostly in their eighties or older, age and leave us, it is a rare blessing to engage with any creative force behind the designs of the time. So in 2017, when a young family took over this impressive but tired home on Victoria's Mornington Peninsula, they were keen to reach architect Karl Fender. As Mid-Century Modern devotees, they understood that reinstating the architectural roots of this house via refurbishment was a delicate task and gaining the blessing of the architect himself would be a validation. In 1973 Fender had been a new-generation protégé of Robin Boyd and aged a mere twenty-three when he completed this commission. A subsequent career trajectory now finds him as founding partner of the prestigious international firm Fender Katsalidis. Suffice it to say, after much work had been completed a social media tag led to a visit from the architect. Arriving with stories and hand-drawn plans, Fender bestowed his approval, much to the relief of the new custodians, who had by this point decided to rechristen the house after the architect himself.

Such are the dimensions of this residence that it radiates a distinct monumentality, welcoming guests up elongated stairs to the double front doors like ever-shrinking Alices in Wonderland. Though relatively unaltered at the time of their purchase, the home presented the owners with more than enough to redress inside and out. Initial investigations revealed asbestos and termite-affected flooring at risk of collapse. Big repairs were in order for the central kitchen which, once structurally sound, was aesthetically rejigged, the white cabinetry and metallic appliances supplanted with warm timber and integrated technology. That said, some technology of the age has been kept in situ to wonderful effect, with children using the original wall-mounted phones for imaginary meetings, while the adults spin Bill Withers on the record player downstairs. The desire to accommodate mobs of guests called for the reconfiguration of the northern room and patio, which previously hosted an enormous freestanding spa (!!), and conversion of the upstairs study into a sixth bedroom.

Architectural and design flourishes once hidden are now celebrated, including the unique bedroom lightboxes and timber lining. 'Occasional' furniture which had plagued every alcove and living area was decamped and far fewer vintage pieces strategically repositioned. This adjustment gracefully allows the building's characteristics, such as bagged brick walls, fixed joinery and soaring windows, to unfurl and reclaim for the resident a pure enjoyment of the space. This considered furniture placement also delineates sections with clear zoning in an otherwise rambling house, providing a gamut of options for sleeping, dining, relaxing or partying.

The visual refurbishment is underpinned by the upgrading of fundamental systems, including hydronic heating, solar panels and septic plumbing, to future-proof for comfort and sustainability. Internally, an uninspiring combination of white gloss tiles and grey carpet was exchanged for new velour carpet in an exacting chartreuse, reasserting the nostalgic 1970s warmth. Earth-toned terrazzo unites the impressive entry, traffic and utility areas across multiple split levels, all the way down to the poolside. And it is indeed here, by the pool, where the thrill of this residence truly radiates. Demolition of a brick cabana, replacement decking, major earthworks and precise landscaping wholly embrace a refurbished azure pool and terrazzo patio, exalting this central courtyard from a neglected resort to a Slim Aarons photoshoot. Here too, the careful deployment of glass pool fencing adheres to regulations without intruding on the fantasy.

To exist, for a little while, in a glamourous Mid-Century Modern universe, Pucci attired, cocktail in hand, is an irresistible draw and one which these owners have wrangled back from an unruly starting point. It is a testament to their vision, dedication to the era and sheer grind that this home regularly hosts fashion shoots and awed guests, their praise and appreciation written on every page of the visitors' book.

Fender House

Karl Fender – Owners

←　A dining table sits beside soaring double-height windows, overlooking the poolside courtyard.

→　Succulents and cacti populate nooks inside and out.

↓　The glorious timber ceilings traverse all levels, providing an overhead patina of natural warmth.

← The kitchen and dining spaces were combined by removing a wall; the freestanding shelf remains, adorned with plants and pottery.

→ The original kitchen aesthetic has been enhanced by new timber joinery and tile so complementary that they feel part of the original build.

Karl Fender–Owners

←   The enormous double doors at the
    entrance make any visitor feel like a
    child, or a shrinking Alice in Wonderland.

↙   Residual 20th-century technology
    remains, allowing for very important
    teleconferencing.

↓   Thoughtful placement of furniture
    assigns incidental gathering spots
    in less well-defined areas.

Karl Fender—Owners

→ Along with the carpet, a light yet warm-toned terrazzo connects the various living spaces.

↘ Once sectioned off from the kitchen by a wall and door, the dining space has been opened up, allowing more casual, intuitive use.

↓ A mid-century glass ashtray remains elegant, long after retirement.

← The bagged brick walls were an original aspect, requiring only a new paint job to refresh.

→ Half-wall windows in all the bedrooms along the second level ensure a constant flow of northern light.

Karl Fender—Owners

Fender House

Location	Bridgeman Downs, Queensland
	Kabi Kabi, Jinibara and Turrbal Country
Original architect	Peter Green & Associates
Renovation date	2020
Renovation architect	Cloud Dwellers
Renovation builder	D Pearce Constructions
Interior design	Cloud Dwellers
Photography	Cathy Schusler

1979

Bismark Blue

Peter Green & Associates–Cloud Dwellers

p. 254 This 'younger' Mid-Century Modernist home was conceived and built by a local architect and has now been beautifully updated by a similarly local architect.

p. 255 The diagonal timber boards, which impart a particular 1970s energy, are having a moment of rediscovery by millennials and younger generations.

← Called 'Bismark', this affecting blue was selected from an older 20th-century range, not unlike Pantone, dubbed 'British Standard' by Resene.

Contour lines representing the rise and fall of land on a map could be, if one chose, similarly applied to graphically reveal the built character of larger Australian cities. Starting centrally with commerce and government in the CBD, the ripple of irregular rings advance, with 19th-century townhouses and workers' cottages leading to the postwar suburban frontlines of the 1940s to 1970s, followed by outer reaches in the unbridled sprawl of the 1990s and 2000s. Each of these lines is infilled with the architecture and landscaping of its age, offering a particular personality to each. Of course, it's the 'middle-ring' suburbs that sit permanently in the eye of a Mid-Century Modern aficionado, be it for house-hunting, a Sunday stroll stickybeak or fruitful hard-rubbish expedition.

Sitting on the furthest mid-century contour of Brisbane, one or two lines further from 1960s enclaves such as Kenmore (see page 206, Kenmore Renovation) sits this lovely late 1970s, two-storey residence. The house was initially purchased by a family who thereafter moved cities but eventually returned to Brisbane to make this residence their forever home. Attracted to the building's warm, era-specific character but needing to rework certain aspects, the owners engaged architect Jason Haigh, of the local firm Cloud Dwellers, to skilfully guide the changes.

The original architect, Peter Green, is not necessarily one of the big names cited in academia and exhibitions, unlike others in this book, but was rather one of the countless local practitioners ensconced within the evolution of Modernist design and the ascendant tastes of the time. The home was beautifully crafted and held a breezy yet shaded beauty typical of the late 1970s Modernist houses built for successful middle-class families that dot this suburban ring.

The main work of the brief, the architect explains, focused on the internal spaces and movement: 'The home was to be made better for the occupants within, not to please passers-by who view it, like an object, from the roadside.' As a middle-aged (rather than elderly) Mid-Century Modern home it is structurally quite sound, so the focus centred on the celebration of the integral materials and overall design, while bringing more light and cohesion. A second stage to sensitively upgrade the exterior in line with the internal is on the books.

The eyes of the observer are drawn to the gorgeous, exposed timber throughout which, for anyone today who is not a multimillionaire, is irreplaceable. Raw brick and the diagonally patterned external cladding similarly extol this 1970s energy, with both elements right now having a well-deserved moment of (re)discovery by the millennial design crowd.

In reimagining the spaces of the ground floor, which holds the living and dining areas, internal walls were demolished to open up the floor space as an entirety. The floor footprint remained the same except for commandeering part of the oversized garage for extra kitchen amenity. A combination of sliding doors and dividing screens reinstated the spaces which now allow life and facility within one pocket yet also interconnection with the whole, as desired.

The most striking aspect of this project and the impetus behind its name is the colour, 'Bismark'. This blue, and similarly chosen jade green, sat among a suggested rainbow from the mid-20th-century-instituted Resene 'British Standard Colour' range, not unlike the Pantone system that is more commonly used today. In academic colour theory, this particular blue speaks to the ochre of the timber in an exact complementary pairing. This use of historical resources for colour exemplifies how a savvy professional works heritage into a new context. Into this mix are injected other bold yet cohesive choices, such as the terrazzo benchtops and minimalist joinery, each working to create a uniquely combined vision in new for old. Much to the joy of the owners, this home resonates with its past yet is boldly situated in the now, and maintains comfort and utility at its heart.

Bismark Blue

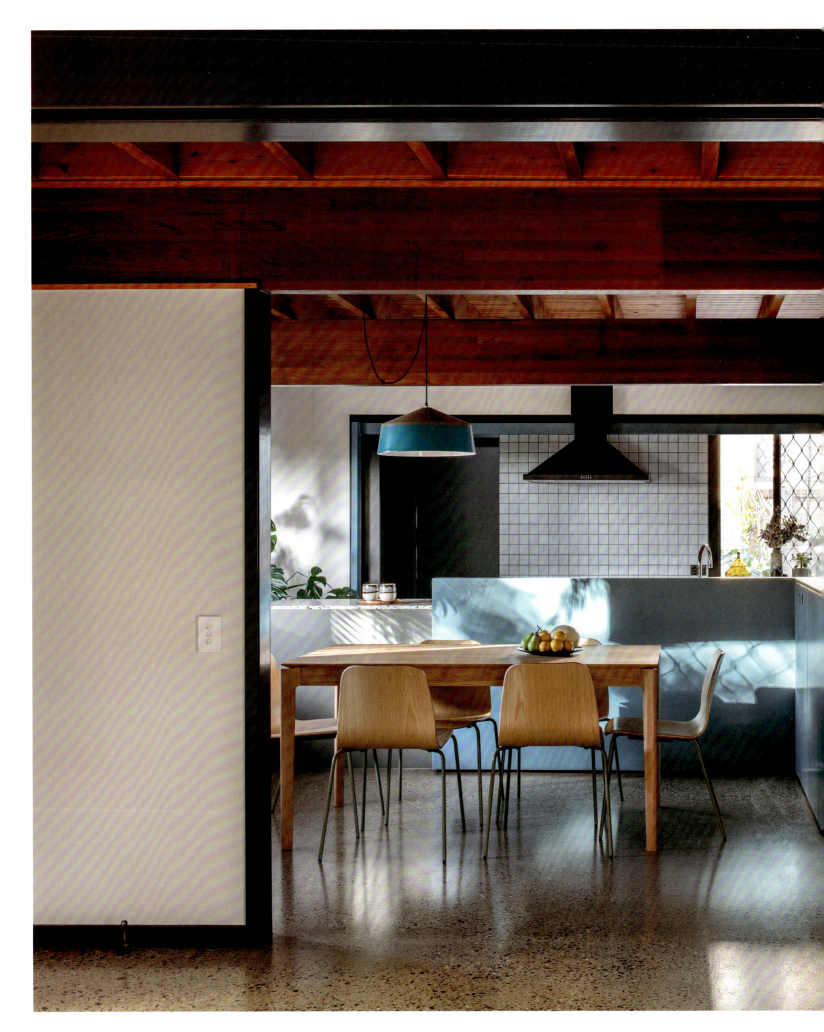

Peter Green & Associates–Cloud Dwellers

↑   New cabinetry, though boldly coloured, is minimalist and clean, almost industrial, in form.

←   The architect removed most walls on the ground floor, redefining the spaces via other means – furniture and sliding doors – to improve useability.

← The specific use of a chunky terrazzo pattern in the benchtops and square mosaic tiles on the walls reference once-daring Mid-Century Modern accents.

→ The home still retains much of its 1970s construction, these windows with their yellow railing midsection a nostalgic example.

Peter Green & Associates–Cloud Dwellers

↑   The colour scheme walks upstairs
    with this light shade.

←   The irreplaceable timber ceilings and
    trusses resonate in a deep ochre hue,
    creating a formal colour partnership
    with the painted blues.

→   Here a lighter jade works with the
    terrazzo in a refreshed bathroom.

← Flexibility of space may see a children's playroom easily converted into a study or spare bedroom as needed.

→ The new partitions incorporate bespoke shelving in alternating blue and unpainted timbers for visual interest.

Peter Green & Associates–Cloud Dwellers

Bismark Blue

House Gezellig
1980s

Location	Warrawee, New South Wales
	Darramuragal Country
Original architect	Unknown
Renovation date	2020
Renovation architect	Studio Prineas
Renovation builder	Element Constructions
Interior design	Studio Prineas
Landscape design	Serenescapes Landscape Design
Styling	Anna Delprat
Photography	Felix Forest

Unknown–Studio Prineas

Unlike all of the other homes in this book, and on this basis a true outlier, House Gezellig was not originally a Mid-Century Modern residence of any formal architectural pedigree and was in fact built in the 1980s. Despite this, pre-renovation it already incorporated Modernist principles of deeply considered functionality and movement, being originally designed for disability access. The otherwise nondescript home with its single-level plan and generous access appealed to an older couple seeking to settle down and enjoy the comings and goings of their family.

These owners, seasoned travellers of lengthy European tenure, already possessed a deep appreciation for Mid-Century Modernism and brought with them selected art and collectibles of the age. A line of cherished KLM in-flight ceramics, Fiesta crockery and an Alexander Calder mobile most certainly needed their own display places. This appreciation combined with the pragmatic attitudes of the owners with regard to function and space conspired to underpin their renovation preferences with a distinctly Mid-Century Modern spirit.

The architects tasked with the renovation, Studio Prineas, held long discussions connecting with their clients, setting out a pathway to help steer choices of a practical but also spiritual nature. The owners were enamoured by and introduced the concept of 'gezellig', a Dutch word that refers to the familial cosiness of warm spaces enjoyed with others, and so it became the guiding theme throughout the works.

The starting point in any renovation of Modernist intent is to assess the environmental requirements, and in this case the architects needed to first address the difficult orientation of the house. Their resolution was to open up the high ceilings by removing the old skylights and inserting larger-scale glazing to capture the sunlight.

To achieve privacy for the large main bedroom and create a new entry walk, expanses of breeze block wall were built. This perfect screening device is concurrently a delightful Mid-Century Modern material aesthetic making a deserved comeback in Australian architecture. Paired with these walls and in a nod to the Modernist desert gardens of Palm Springs, formal pockets of low-maintenance grasses and succulents were laid alongside stone pathways and floating lines of pavers.

Some design cues were expanded to reference the existing character of the home, including the gorgeous two-tone in-fill wardrobes. The interior craftsmanship in other sections embodies a specifically evocative echo of a Mid-Century Modern aesthetic, such as the silver travertine flooring (a Mies van der Rohe favourite) and exquisite crosscut walnut joinery for built-in seating, bedhead and martini bar. Elsewhere, construction of the centrepiece stone fireplace to emulate those found in Seidler's homes, a client favourite, became a point of devotion requiring client trips to the right quarry, for the right coloured stone, just like Harry's.

At the completion of the renovation project and always part of the brief was the painting of an abstract wall mural, another Mid-Century Modern flourish. Devised in-house by the architect's office using the breeze block pattern, it was brushed in collectively as a celebration between owners, architects and builder. This mural signified a finale to a successful collaboration of highly self-possessed owners and empathetic, creative professionals. Tasked to embed a deeper Modernist ethos into a compatible though unremarkable building, the architects met the objective, resulting in a residence of understated yet beautifully considered spaces.

House Gezellig

→ A fireplace of quarried stone emulating the one found in Harry Seidler's Rose Seidler House was a specific feature desired by the owners.

271

← The display of the owners' collection of vintage crockery and a request for a built-in martini bar steered choices for joinery in the kitchen and elsewhere.

→ The silver travertine flooring that completes the dining and living spaces was a material favourite of another Mid-Century Modern legend, Mies van der Rohe.

↑   In-fill wardrobes in cream and dark timber, a delightful hangover from the original home, were expanded into an elegant feature in the bedroom.

↘   Stone surfaces are repeated here, appearing with mosaic Japanese tile in a new bathroom.

→   The ultimate Mid-Century Modern bedroom aesthetic: sleek built-in bedhead and shelving in stunning cross-cut timber. The era-recall resonance is topped off with a Marset Dipping Light.

House Gezellig

↑ The geometric mural on the wall of the outdoor dining area, another nod to Mid-Century Modernism, was painted by the architect, the builder and the owners together upon completion of the project.

→ The success of this considered renovation lies in the functionality of the home, updated in sincere deference to Mid-Century Modernist ideals and styling.

Unknown–Studio Prineas

House Gezellig

Directory

Architects and designers

8 Squared
8squared.com.au

Adriana Hanna

Architects Ink
architectsink.com

Cloud Dwellers
cloud-dwellers.com.au

Frank Designs
frankdesigns.com.au

Kennedy Nolan
kennedynolan.com.au

KIN Architects
kinarchitects.com.au

Lian
lian.com.au

MRTN Architects
mrtn.com.au

Nino Sydney

Norwood Designs

Ohlo Studio
ohlostudio.com

Pop Architecture
poparchitecture.com.au

Preston Lane
prestonlane.com.au

Simon Pendal Architect
simonpendal.com

Studio 101 Architects
studio101.com.au

Studio Gorman
studiogorman.com

Studio Prineas
studioprineas.com.au

Trace Architects
tracearchitects.com.au

Wilko Architecture
wilkoarchitecture.com.au

WOWOWA Architecture & Interiors
wowowa.com.au

Photographers

Alicia Taylor
aliciataylorphotography.com

Ben Clement
benclement.world

Black and White Real Estate Marketing
(BWRM) Geelong
bwrm.com

Cathy Schusler
cathyschusler.com

Christopher Frederick Jones
cfjphoto.com.au

Derek Swalwell
derekswalwell.com

Felix Forest
felixforest.com

Jack Lovel
jacklovel.com

Jacqui Turk
jacquiturk.com.au

Martina Gemmola
gemmola.com

Prue Ruscoe
prueruscoe.com

Robert Frith
acorn.com.au

Sam Noonan
samnoonan.com.au

Sean Fennessy
seanfennessy.com.au

Simon Whitbread
simonwhitbread.com.au

Tim Shaw
shawphotography.com.au

Willem-Dirk du Toit
willem-dirk.com

Further reading

Austin, Fiona, and Simon Reeves, *Beaumaris Modern 2*, Black Inc. Books, Melbourne, 2022.

Austin, Fiona, Simon Reeves and Alison Alexander, *Beaumaris Modern: Modernist Homes in Beaumaris*, Melbourne Books, Melbourne, 2018.

Brockhoff, Fiona, *With Nature: Garden Design by Fiona Brockhoff*, Hardie Grant Books, Richmond, Vic., 2022.

Decorative Art: The Studio Yearbook, anthology series produced annually from 1908 to 1980 by various editors, Studio Vista.

Jackson, Davina, *Australian Architecture: A History*, Allen & Unwin, Sydney, 2022.

Lewi, Hannah, and Philip Goad, *Australia Modern: Architecture, Landscape and Design*, Thames & Hudson Australia, Port Melbourne, Vic., 2019.

McCartney, Karen, *50/60/70 Iconic Australian Houses: Three Decades of Domestic Architecture*, Murdoch Books, Crows Nest, NSW, 2007.

O'Callaghan, Judith, and Charles Pickett, *Designer Suburbs: Architects and Affordable Homes in Australia*, NewSouth Publishing, Sydney, 2012.

Practical Guide to Home Landscaping, Reader's Digest Association, Surry Hills, NSW, 1973.

Sunset Reference books for building, gardening, cooking, hobbies and travel. Various titles published during the Lane Publishing ownership period at Menlo Park, Calif., USA (approx. 1951–80.)

Artwork credits

Page 10   Eliza Gosse, *70 Reigate Road, 1979*, 2019, gouache on paper, 30 x 21 cm.

Page 21   Samsung television screensaver: William Turner painting.

Pages 50–51   Samsung television screensaver: Holly Coulis, *Lemons In, Lemons Out, of Vase*.

Page 71   Henry Curchod, *Mask Time*.

Page 89   Kaff-eine, print.

Page 92   Violet Parkhurst, Californian seascape print.

Page 104   Michael Cusack, *Ashmore*, 2019, mixed media on poly cotton, 46 x 38 cm (right); and *Saura*, 2019, mixed media on poly cotton, 90 x 120 cm (left).

Page 110   Nunzio Miano, *Warrior*.

Page 112   Isabelle DeKline, *Sensation*.

Page 113   Annette Russell.

Page 121   Ada Bird Petyarre, *Arnkerrthe Mountain Devil Dreaming*, 2000.

Page 146   Virginia Hodgkinson.

Page 150   Sara Willet (dot painting).

Page 153   Artist unknown, original oil painting c. 1960s.

Page 154   Karen Goodall, *Woman washing*.

Page 155   Virginia Hodgkinson (heads at top).

Page 156   Heather Stewart, *Zeus*, 2012, graphite on cartridge, 92 x 144 cm.

Page 158   Virginia Hodgkinson, *Figure 1* and *Figure 2* (above bed); Jordy Kerwick (painting at left).

Page 162   Zndnek Gruner, *Monteparnais Paris* (back wall).

Page 165   Sarah Keighery, *Blue Monochrome* (left); Ron Robertson Swann, Billy Gruner and Sarah Goffman, *Collective Polychrome* (right).

Page 166   Zndnek Gruner, *Roma*.

Page 168   Zndnek Gruner, *Sancho Panza and Errant Knight*.

Page 172   Kasper Raglus, *Call Out*.

Page 176   Otis Hope Carey, *GAAGAL 5*, acrylic on canvas, 100 x 100 cm.

Page 178   Caroline Walls, *I am a Mother*.

Page 186   Merrick Belyea, *Mosman Bay*, 2019, oil on board, 92 x 91.5 cm.

Page 189   Traianos Pakioufakis, *Post, Chania*, 2018.

Page 191   Traianos Pakioufakis, *Parmigiano-Reggiano*, 2012 (middle image); Traianos Pakioufakis, *Coastal, Chania (Cool)*, (top image).

Page 193   Ben Hosking.

Page 198   Naata Nungurrayi.

Page 200   Minnie Pwerle (left).

Page 201   Matte Stephens.

Page 205   Naata Nungurrayi.

Page 218   Paul Williams (right).

Pages 220, 221   Ita Tipungwuti, *Pukamani*.

Pages 222–223   Zoe Grey, *#6 Reminisce*, 2021, oil on board, 122 x 100 cm.

Page 224   Samsung television screensaver: William Turner painting.

Pages 230, 236   Slim Aarons, *Poolside Glamour*, print of photograph.

Pages 233, 237   Elizabeth Sullivan, *Happy Days*.

Page 239   Evi O, *Gia*, 23 x 17.5 cm.

Page 244   Chris Turnham, *Monstera Deliciosa* (top).

Page 247   House plan drawn by Karl Fender.

Page 250   Friends With You, *Friendship Flag* (left).

Page 252   Derek Swalwell, *Goldstein House*.

Page 262   Abie Loy Kemarre, *Medicine Leaf*.

Acknowledgements

'Rank newbie' is the most applicable term to describe my level of experience in publishing when I was first approached to pitch, then build this book from scratch. My rather cavalier acceptance of such an exciting offer ignited more than a year of unforeseen grind: research, writing, editing, emails, annual leave requests, early starts, sequestered weekends, goodwill expenditure and, more specifically, the great and selfless support of many.

First, a thank you to the architects and designers who generously gave their time (and some secrets), gladly providing a window into their creative minds and machinations. Forget the saying that you should never meet your heroes – in this instance, it was a wonderful experience.

To all the owners, past and present, who continue to open their houses and lives to us gawkers, thank you. Your appreciation of Mid-Century Modernism, manifested within your beautiful homes after so much personal toil, is what keeps this architecture alive and viable in this country. My gratitude for that is immense.

This is ultimately a photography book and without excellent, professional images, works of domestic architecture would never be widely seen and their legacy readily lost. The participation and unfathomable goodwill of the photographers who have contributed images to this book – as well as those who respectfully chose not to – will never be forgotten. It is with admiration I thank you for your works and for an education in protecting one's art and livelihood.

A huge debt of gratitude to Paulina de Laveaux at Thames & Hudson, who plucked me from the online circus and made me an author and who, along with editors Mary Mann and Eugenie Baulch, steered me through the entire process with nothing but warm encouragement. Thanks also to the book's designer, Claire Orrell, who transformed this collection of images and writing into a sleek reality.

A little salute to my online family, the supporters and promoters of Modernist Australia in all its forms, but from the early days especially: Tim Ross, Marcus Lloyd Jones at Modern House Co, Martin and Louise McIntosh at Outré Gallery, Lucy Feagins at The Design Files, the Beaumaris Modern mob and the indomitable Simon Reeves.

To my sisters, who gave of their houses and time to accommodate 'The Book™' in a concurrent season of greater family flux, renovations and covid: thanks, loves. To the rest of my family and my friends, you can finally see it now.

Most importantly a big, heartfelt embrace to my daughters, who never once complained about my attentions being drawn elsewhere, and Pete, a rock unlike any other, who despite his own hectic work and art demands underpinned this entire process with encouragement, coffee and bowling afternoons.

First published in Australia in 2023
by Thames & Hudson Australia Pty Ltd
11 Central Boulevard, Portside Business Park
Port Melbourne, Victoria 3207
ABN: 72 004 751 964

First published in the United Kingdom in 2024
by Thames & Hudson Ltd
181a High Holborn
London WC1V 7QX

First published in the United States
of America in 2024
by Thames & Hudson Inc.
500 Fifth Avenue
New York, New York 10110

The New Modernist House ©
Thames & Hudson Australia 2023

Text © Patricia Callan

Thames & Hudson Australia wishes to
acknowledge that Aboriginal and Torres Strait
Islander people are the first storytellers of
this nation and the traditional custodians
of the land on which we live and work. We
acknowledge their continuing culture and pay
respect to Elders past, present and future.

ISBN 978-1-760-76326-8
ISBN 978-1-76076-409-8 (U.S. edition)

 A catalogue record for this
book is available from the
National Library of Australia

British Library Cataloguing-in-Publication Data
A catalogue record for this book is available
from the British Library

Library of Congress Control Number
2023937136

Front cover:
Kagan House by Anatol Kagan (1953)
and Kennedy Nolan (2019)
Back cover, top:
Frankston House by Clarke Hopkins
Clarke (1963) and MRTN Architects (2019)
Back cover, bottom:
Fender House by
Karl Fender (1973) and owners (2018)
Photographed by Derek Swalwell

Design: Claire Orrell
Editing: Eugenie Baulch
Project manager: Mary Mann
Printed and bound in China by
C&C Offset Printing Co. Ltd

FSC® is dedicated to the promotion of
responsible forest management worldwide.
This book is made of material from FSC®-
certified forests and other controlled sources.

Be the first to know about our new releases,
exclusive content and author events by visiting
thamesandhudson.com.au
thamesandhudson.com
thamesandhudsonusa.com